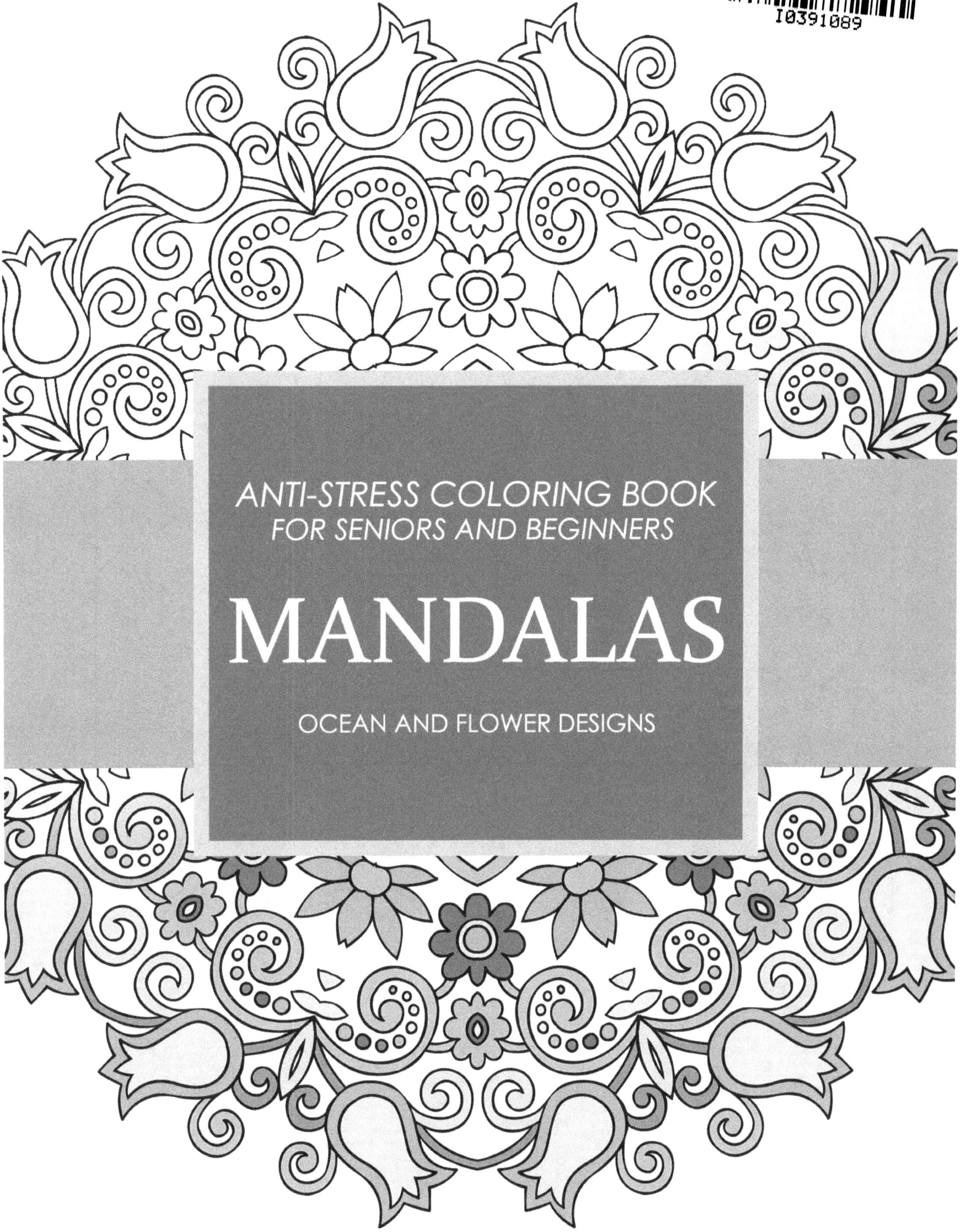

ANTI-STRESS COLORING BOOK
FOR SENIORS AND BEGINNERS

MANDALAS

OCEAN AND FLOWER DESIGNS

TEST YOUR COLOR

TEST YOUR COLOR

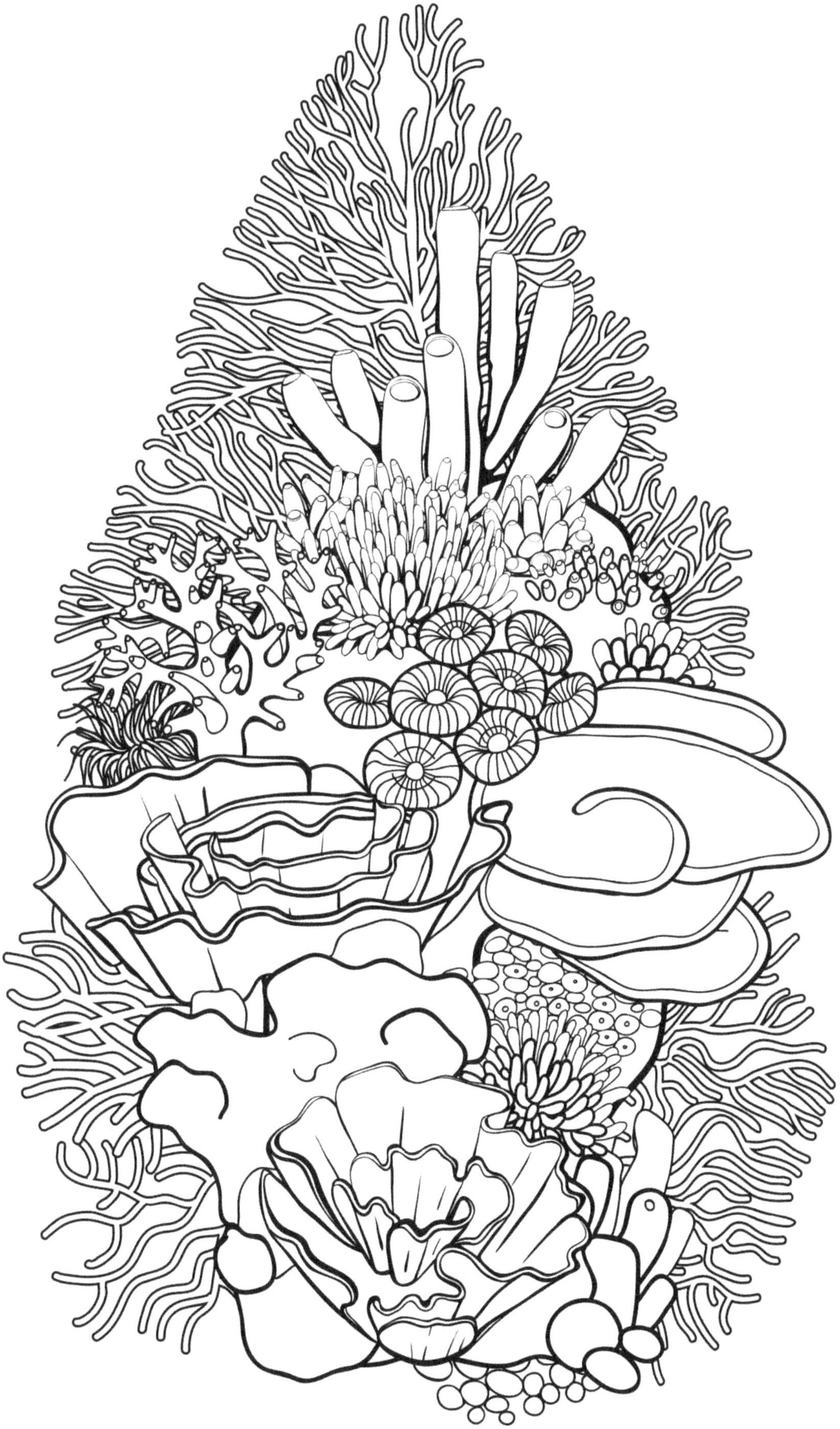

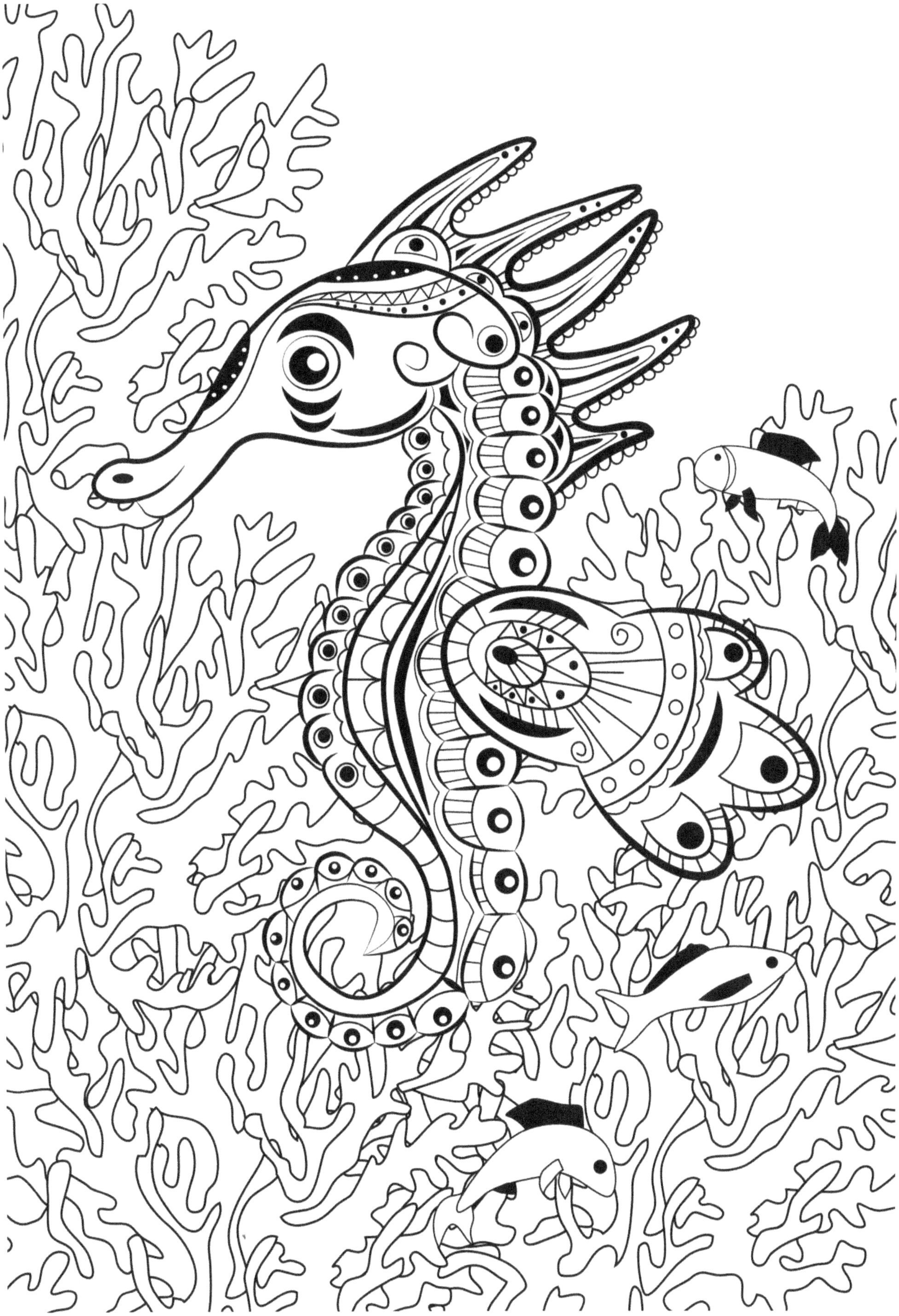

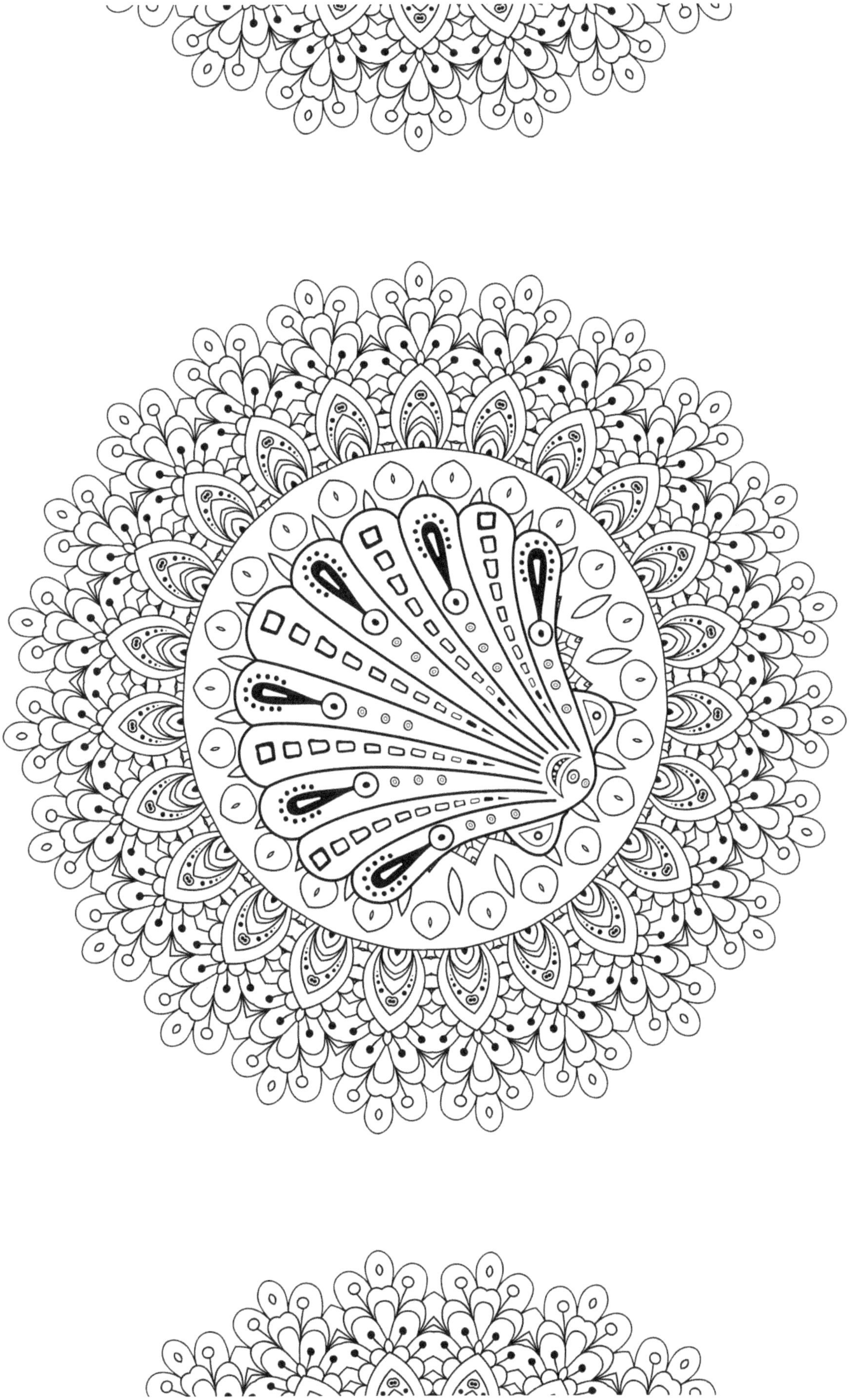

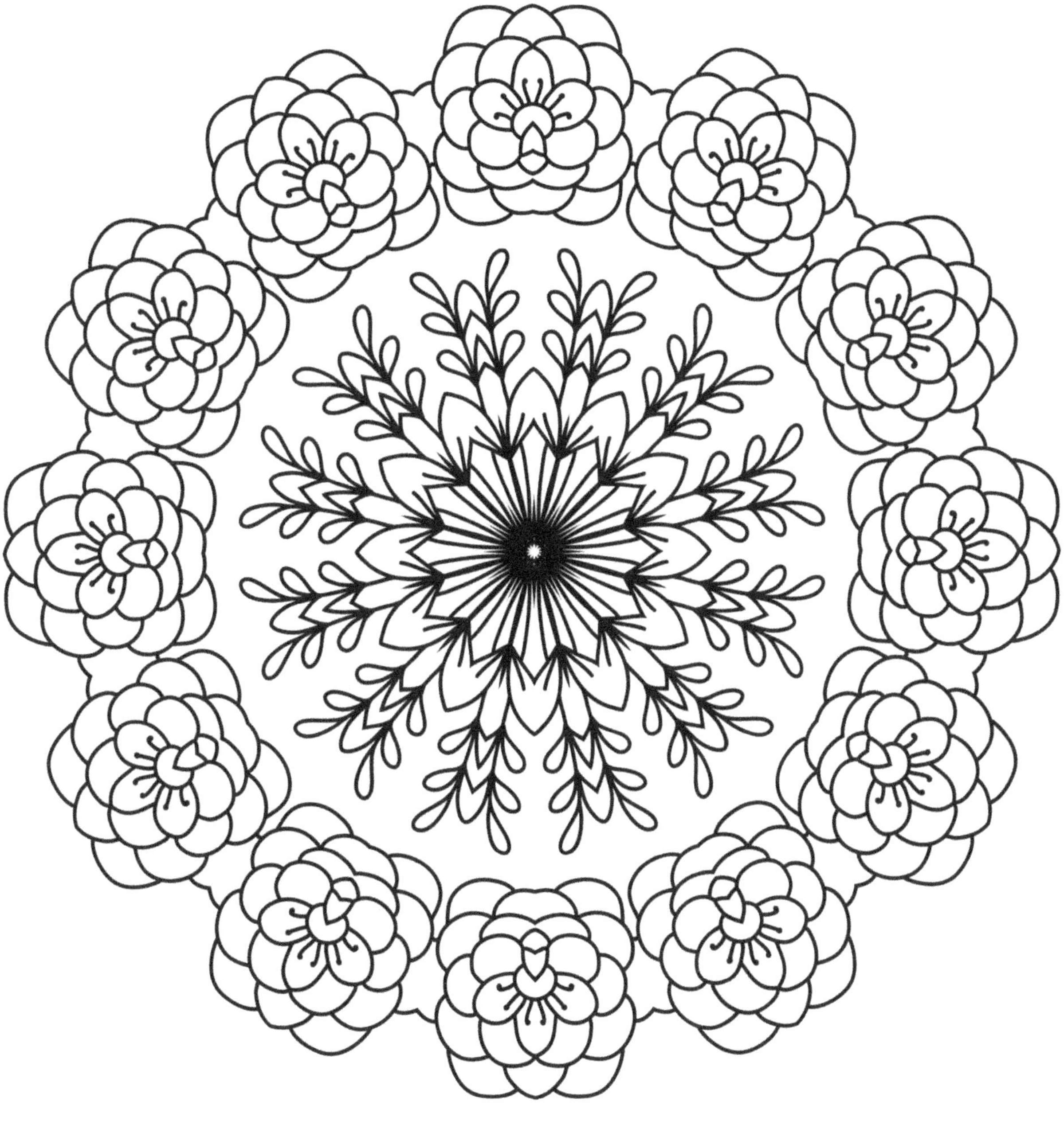

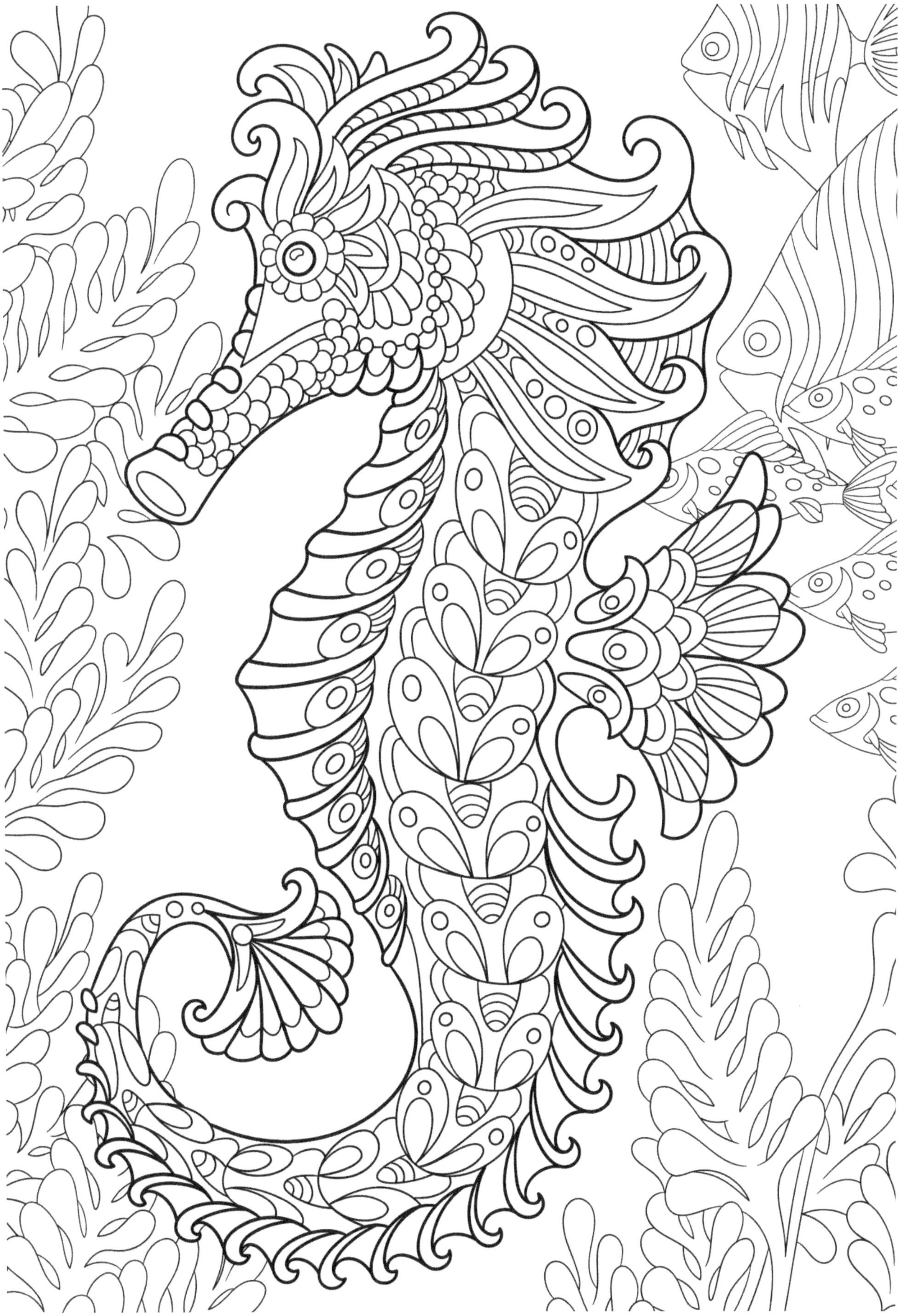

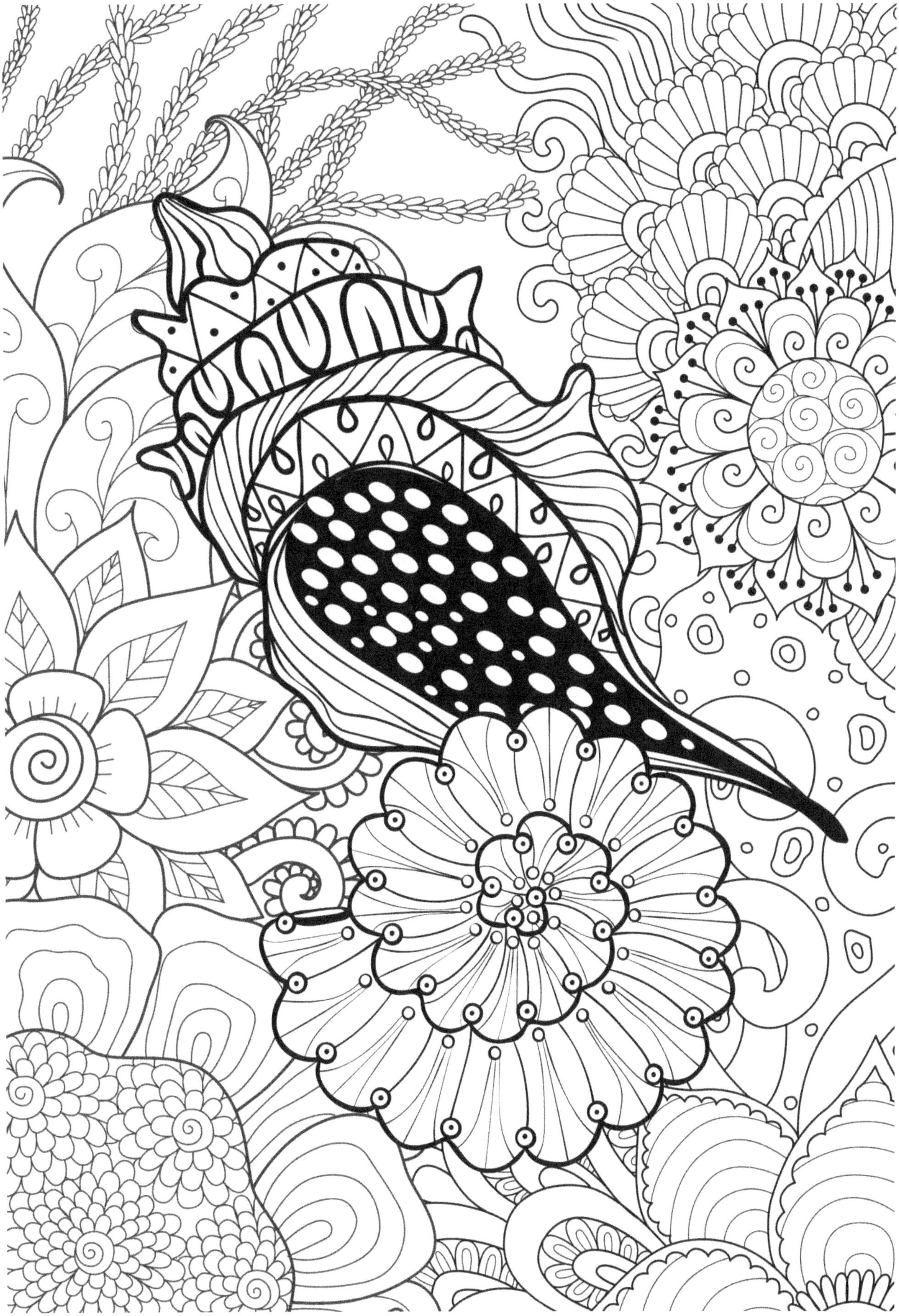

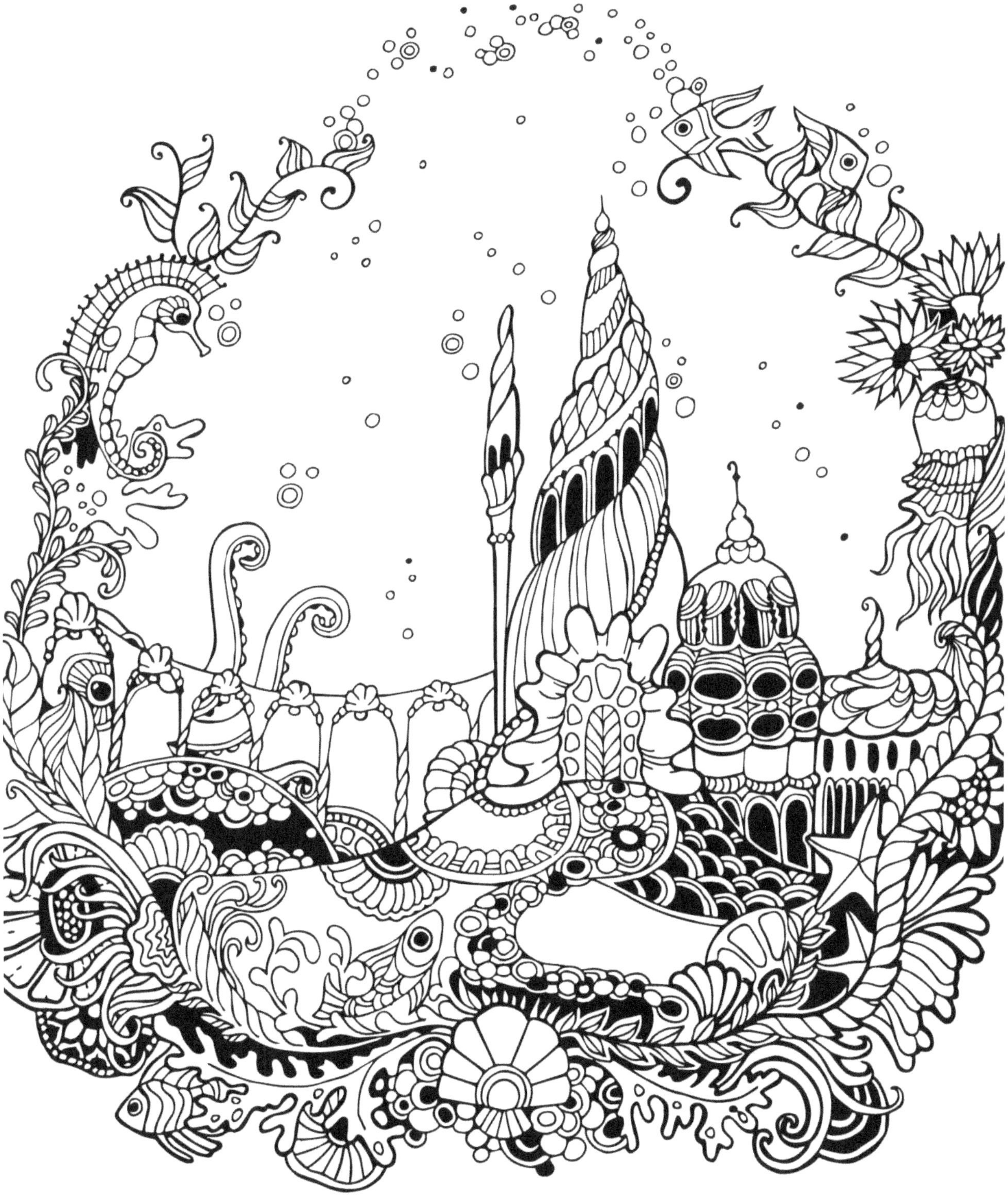

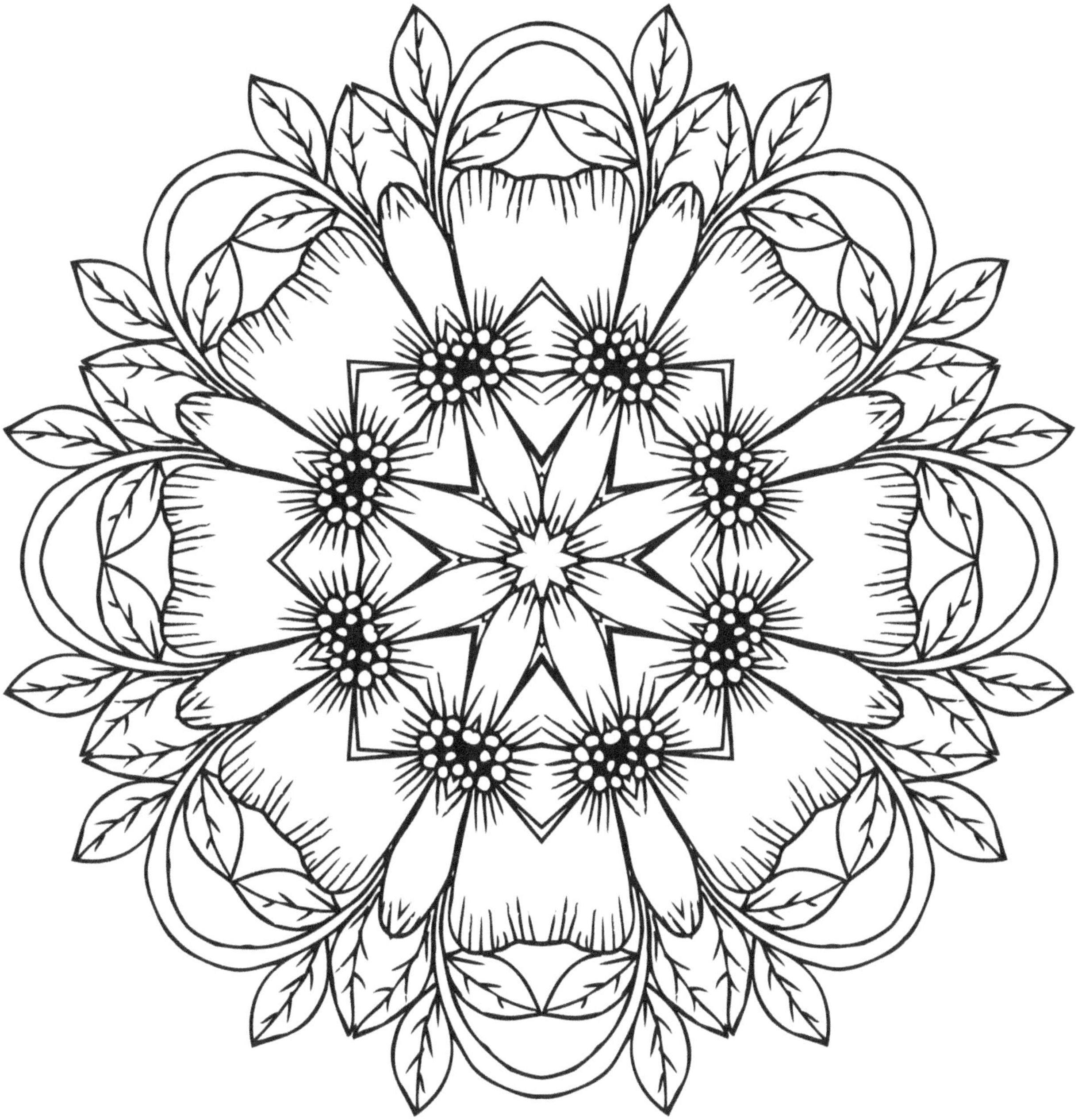

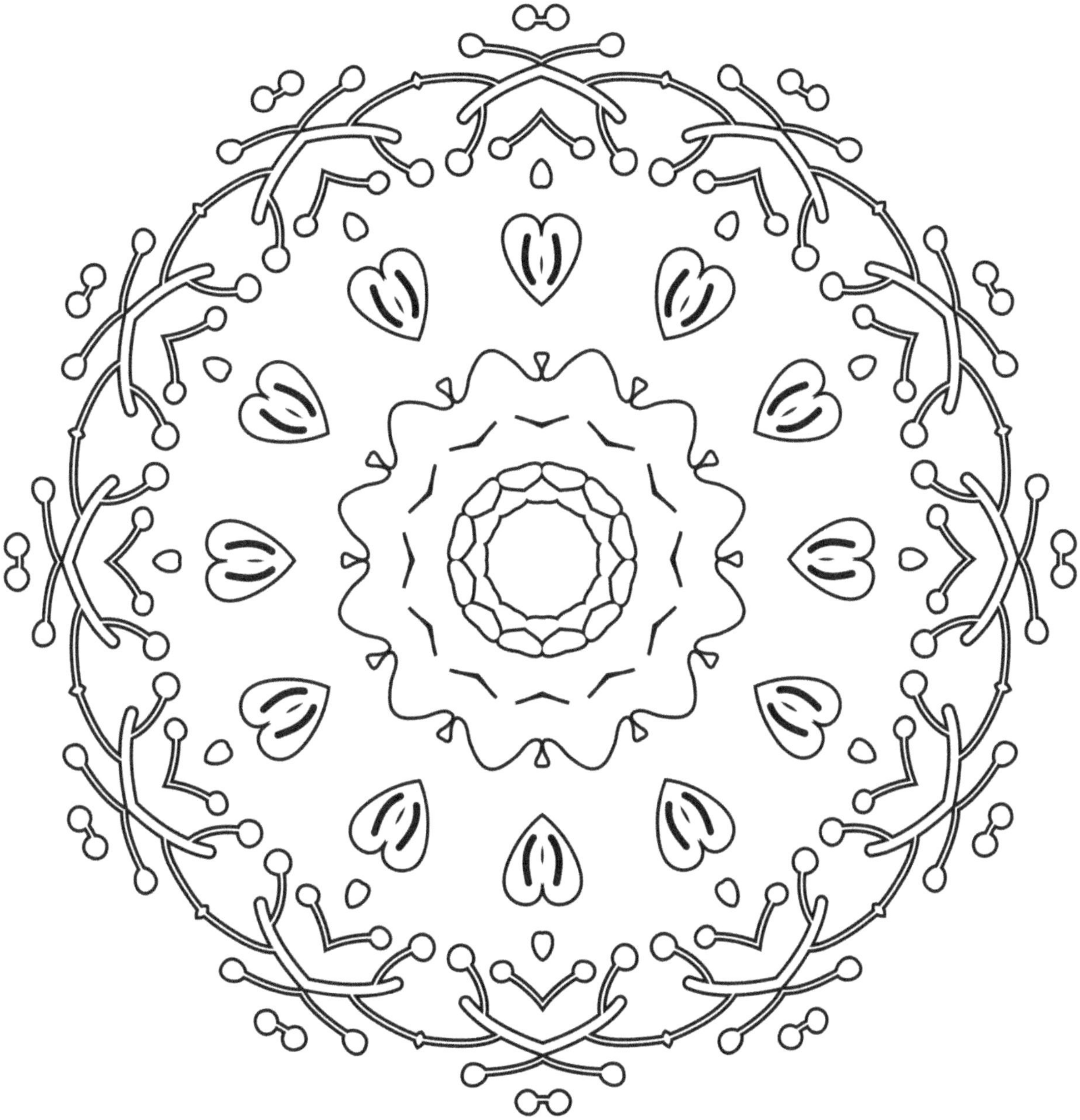

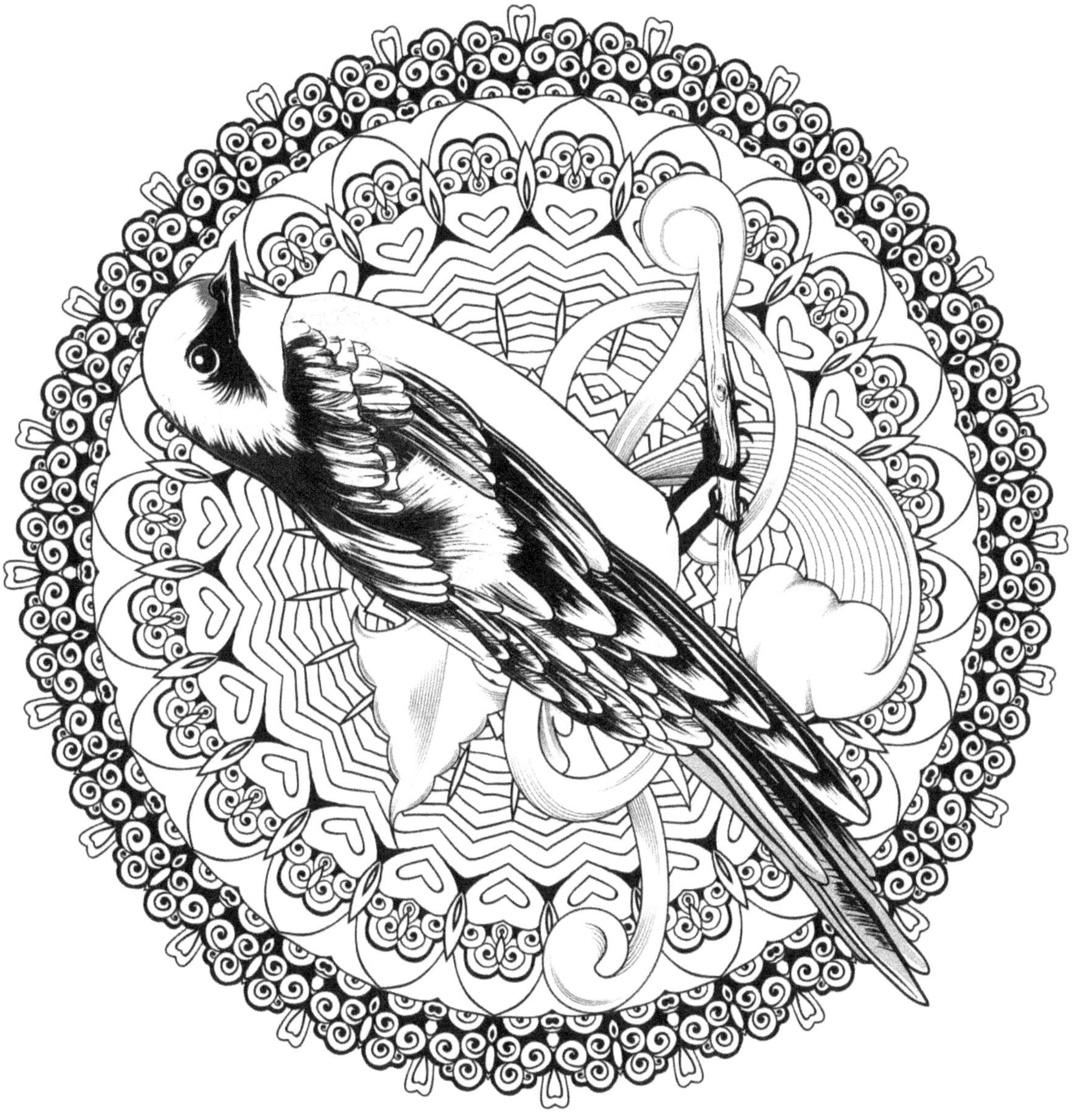

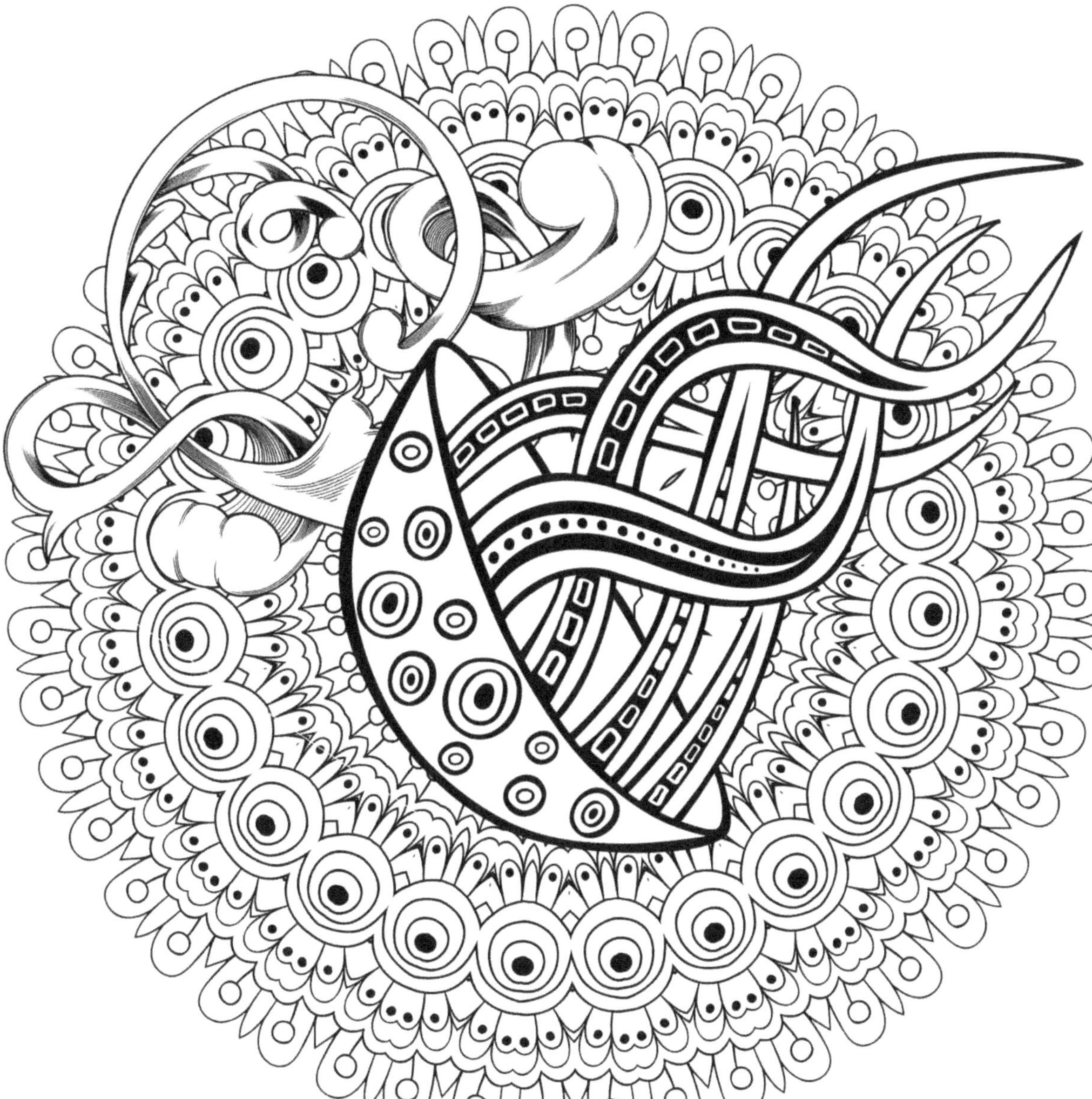

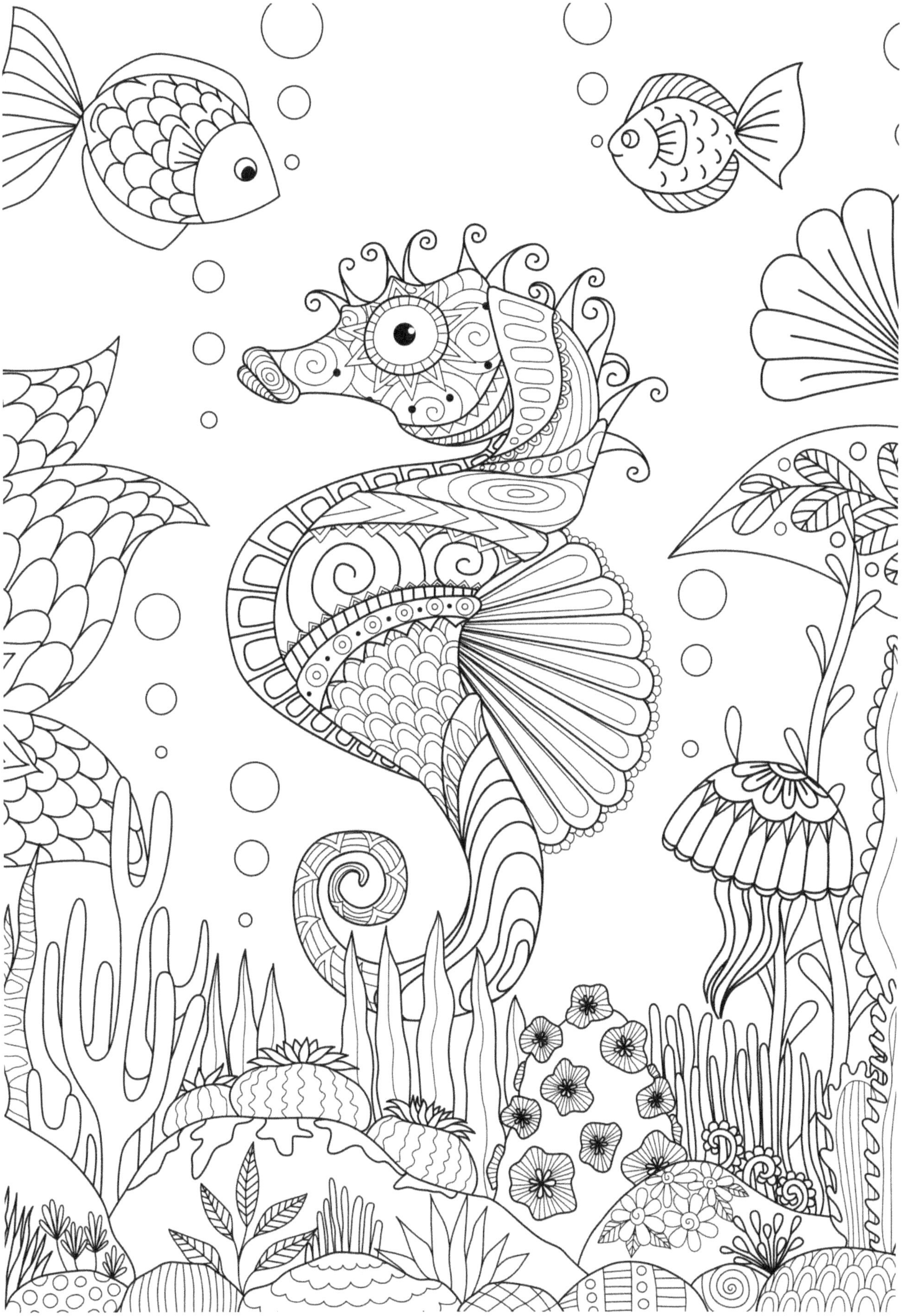

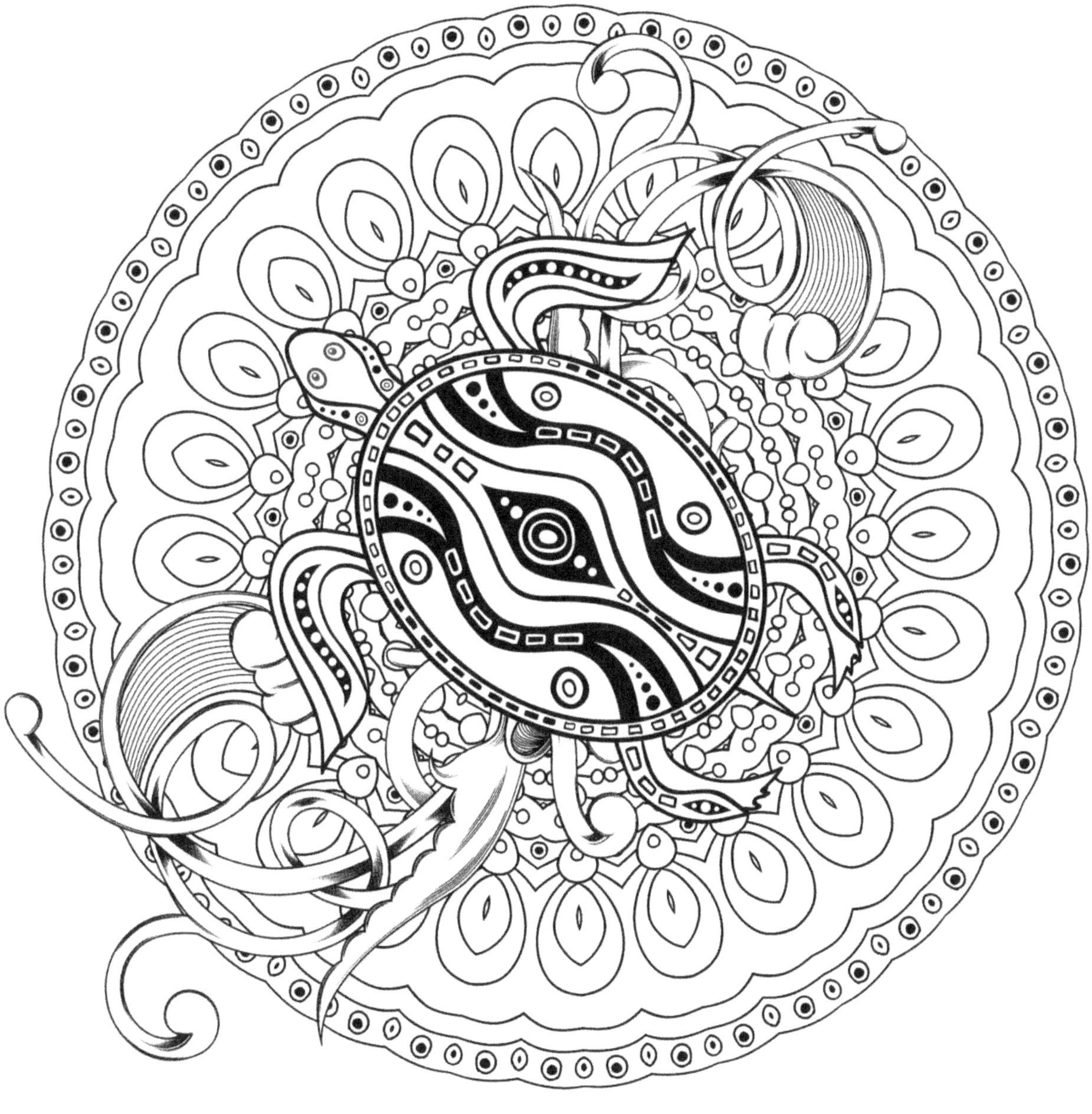

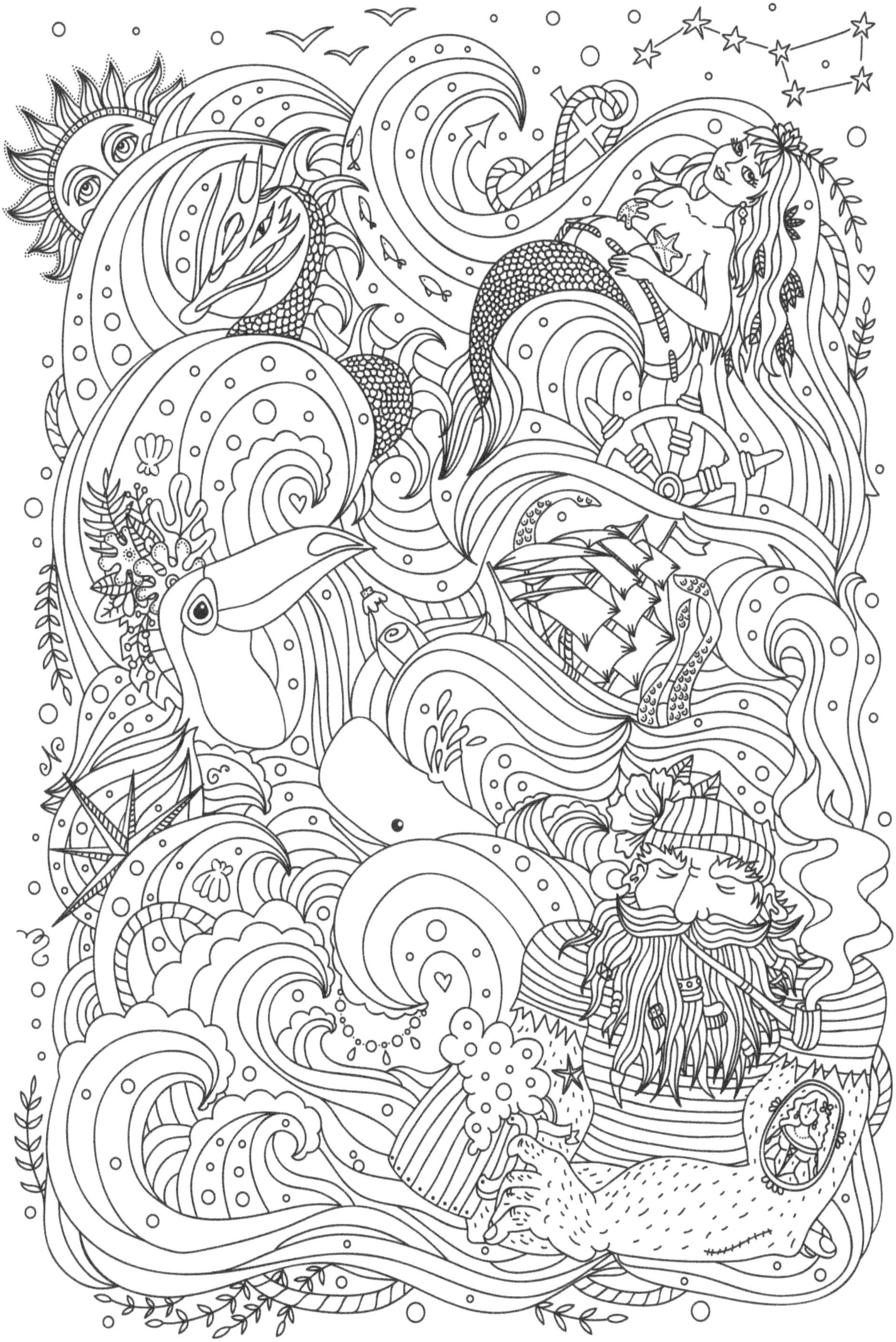

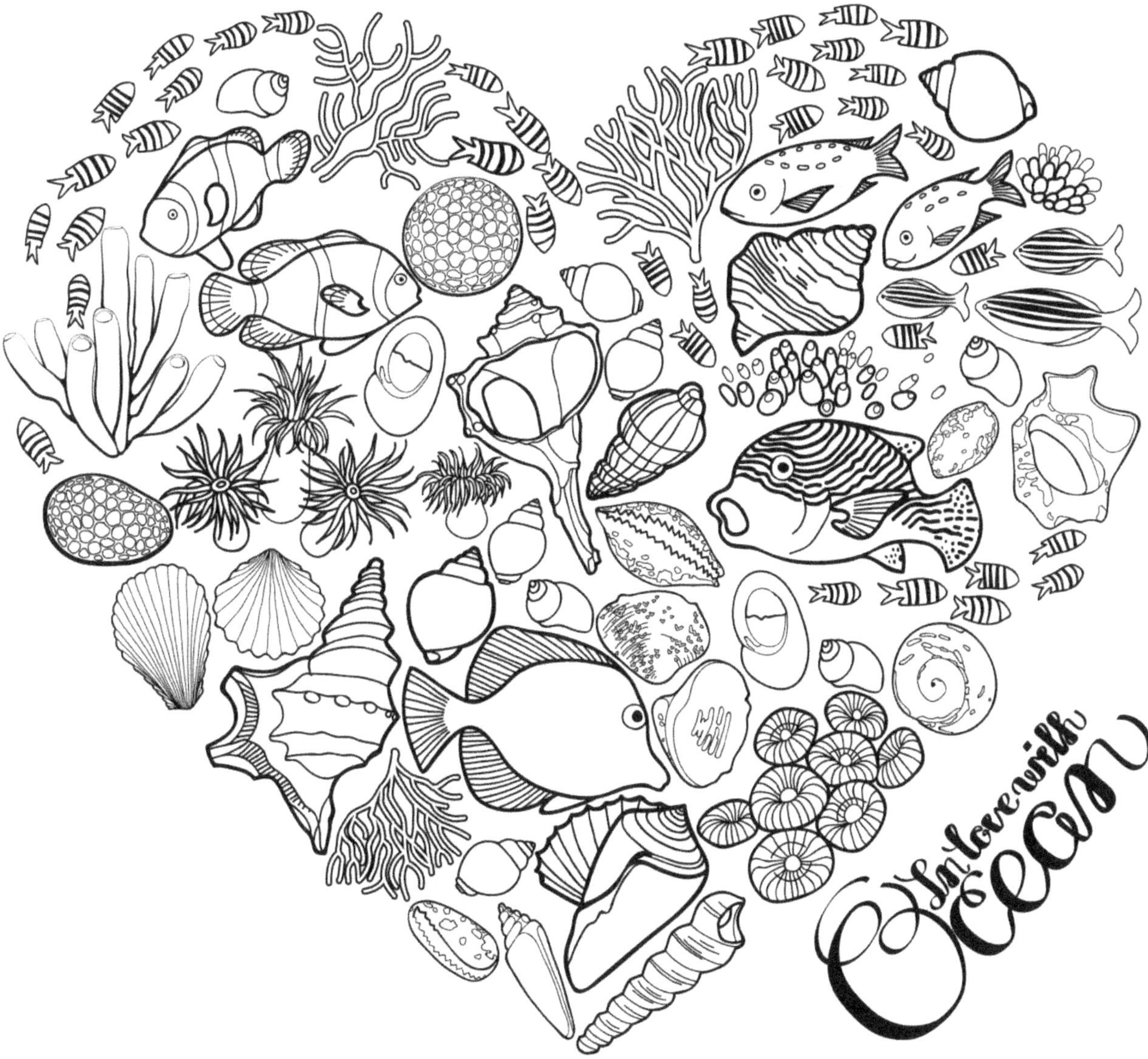
In love with
Ocean

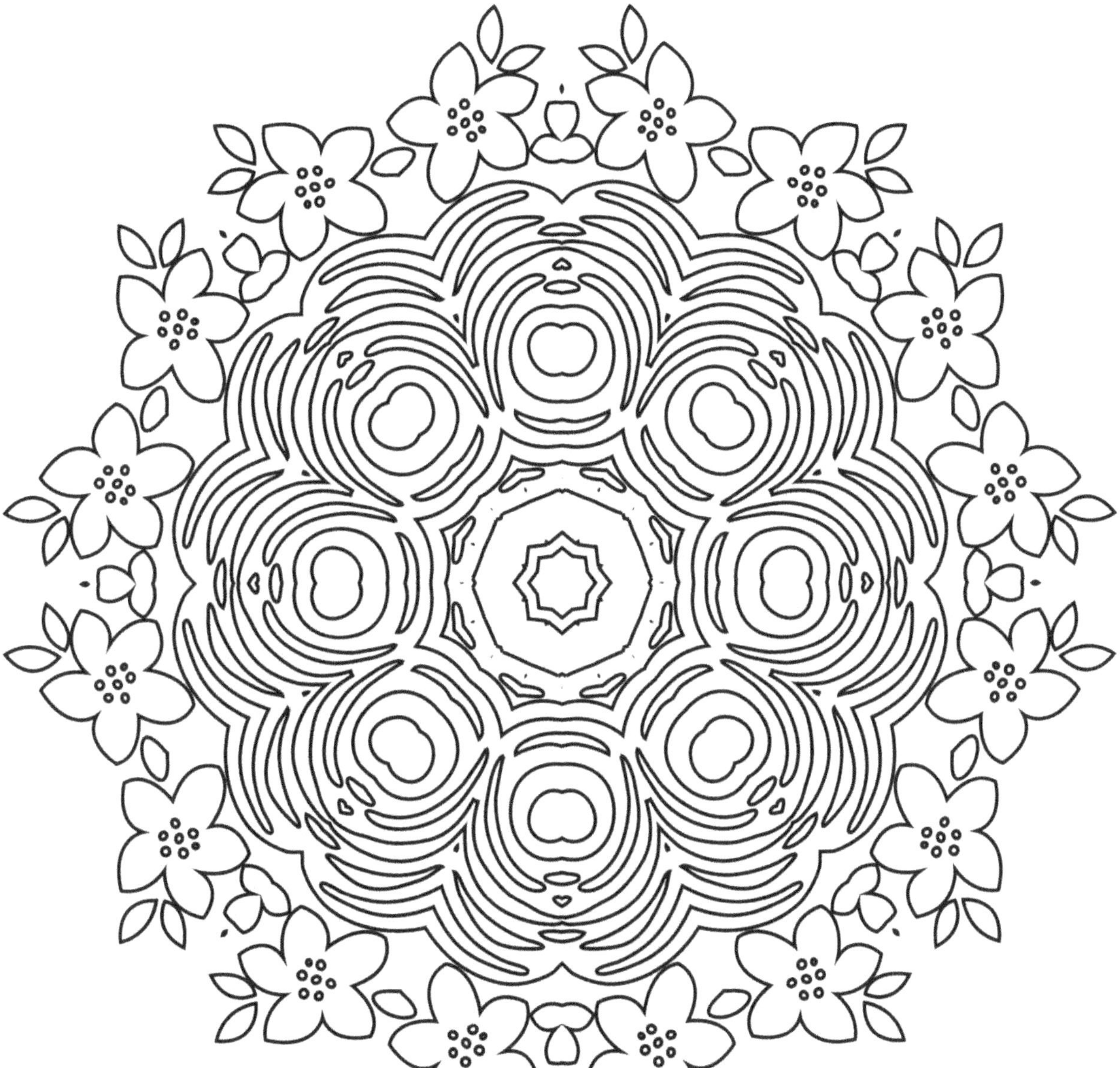

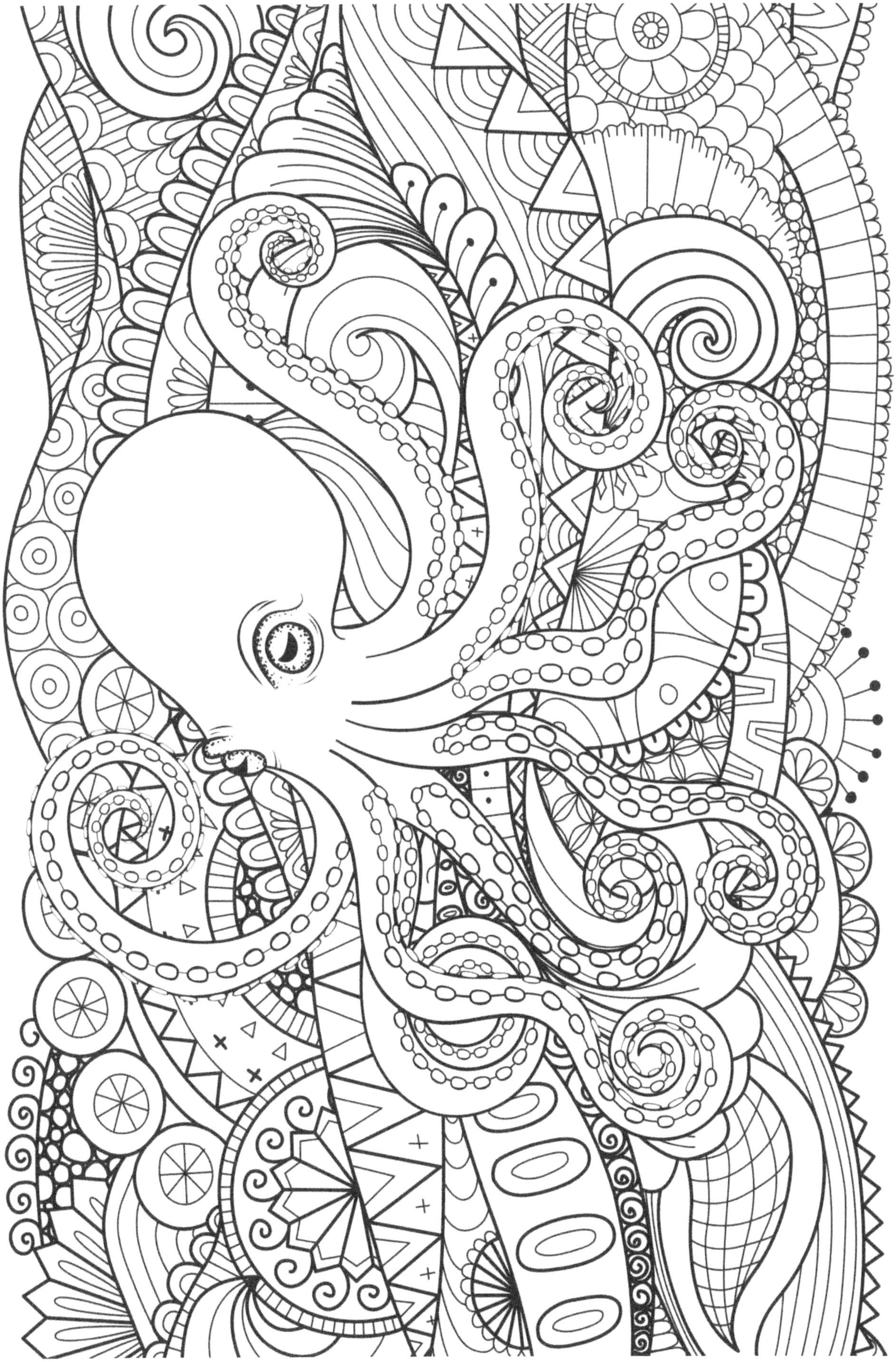

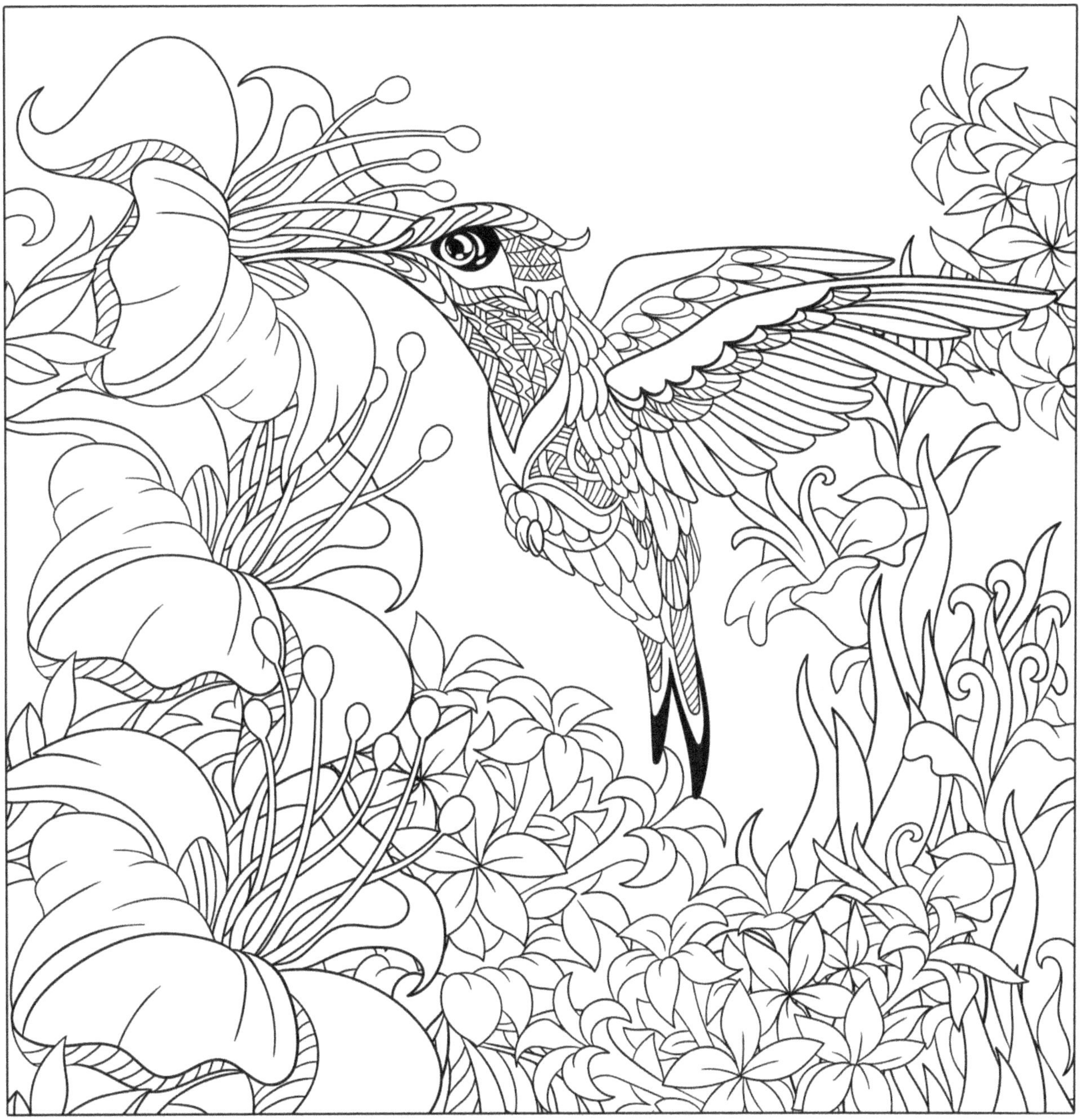

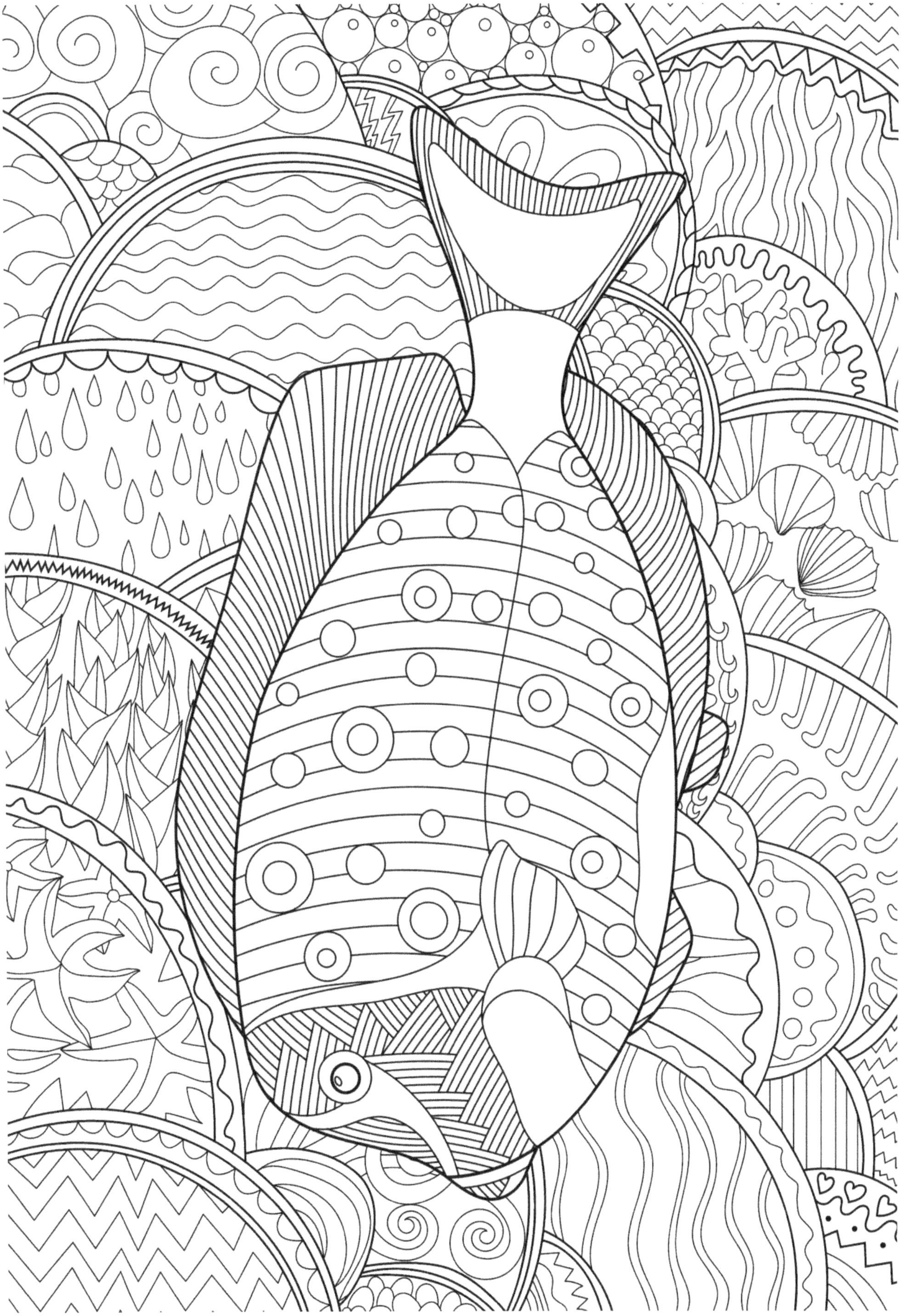

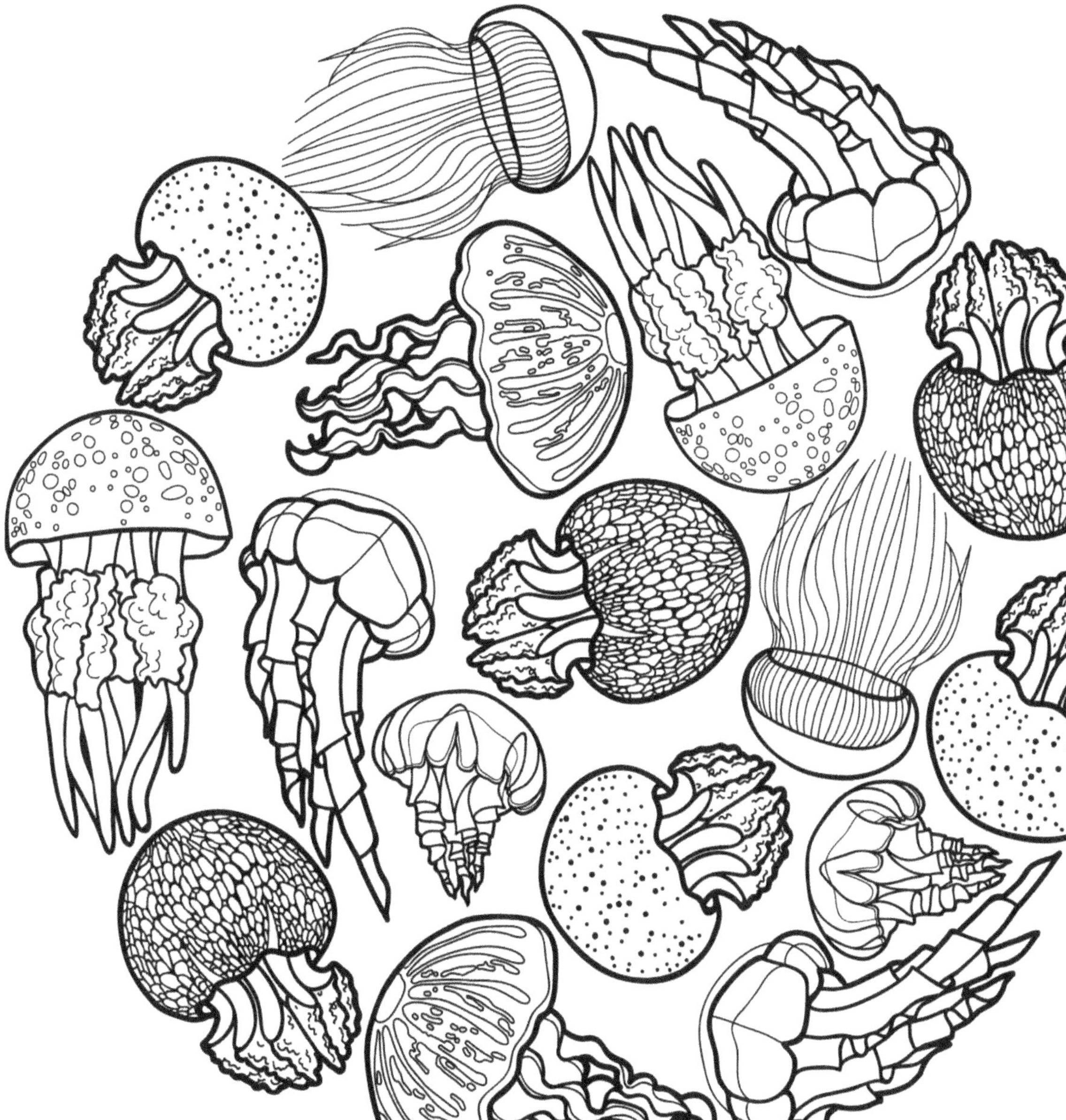

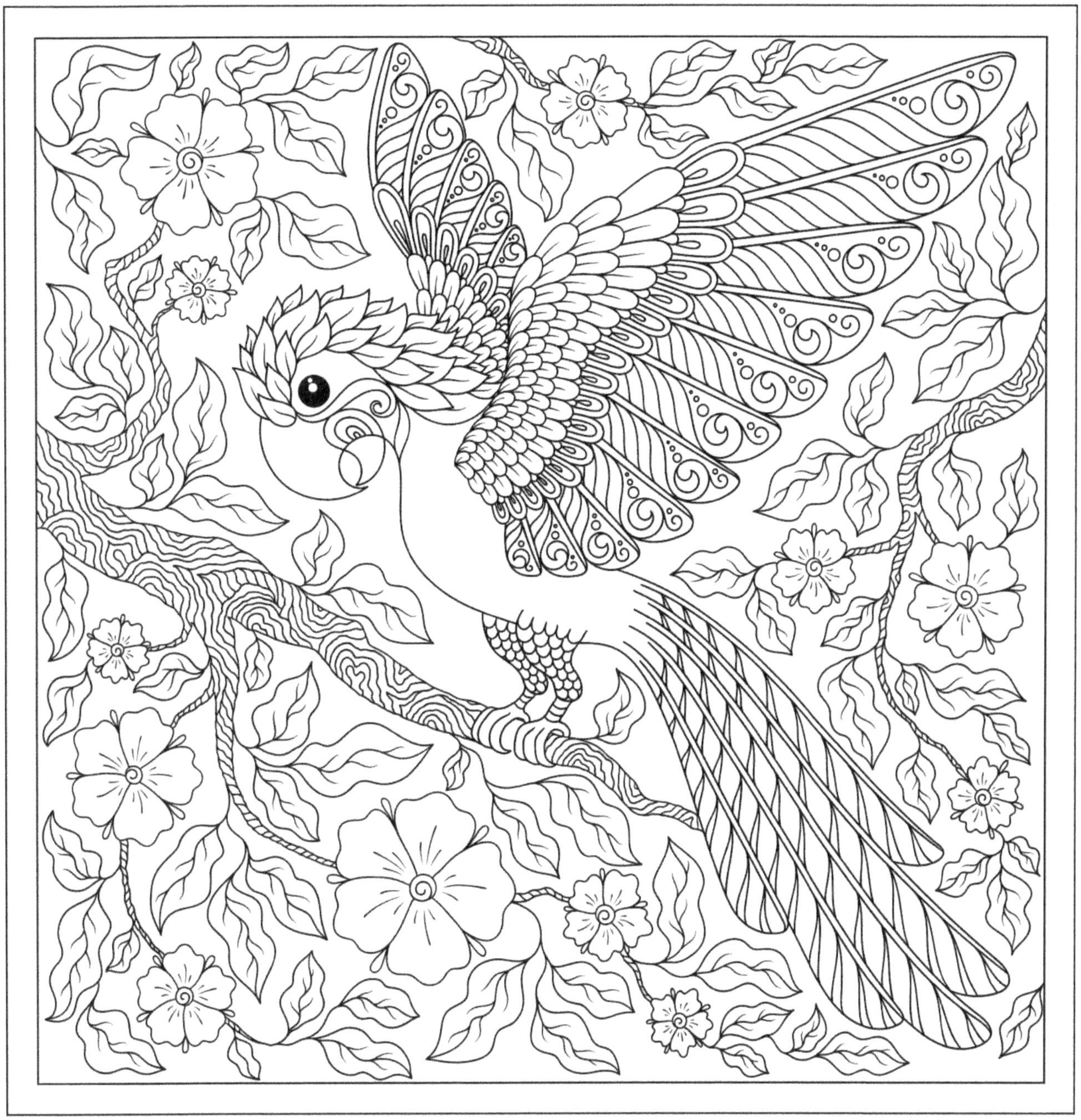

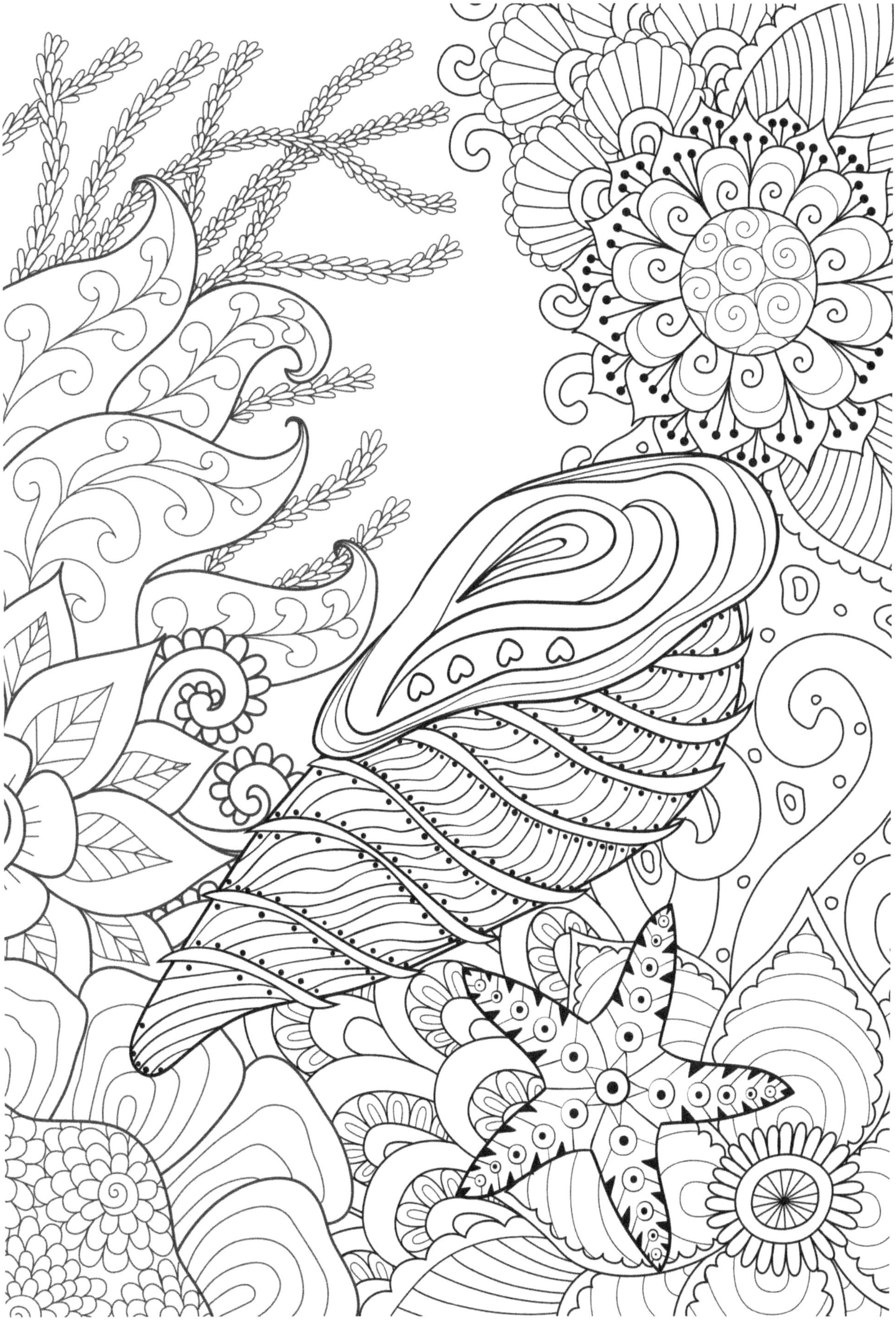

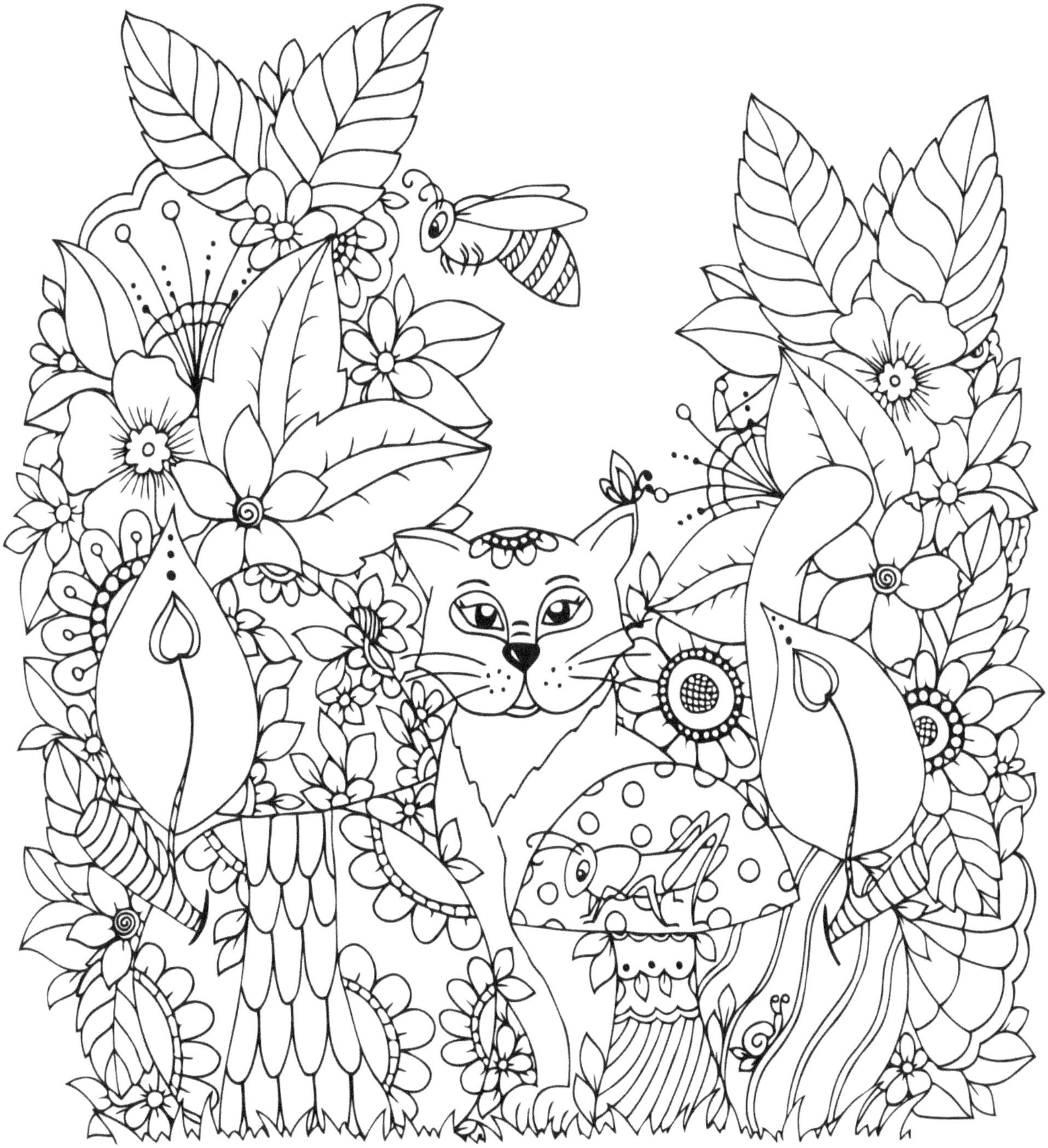

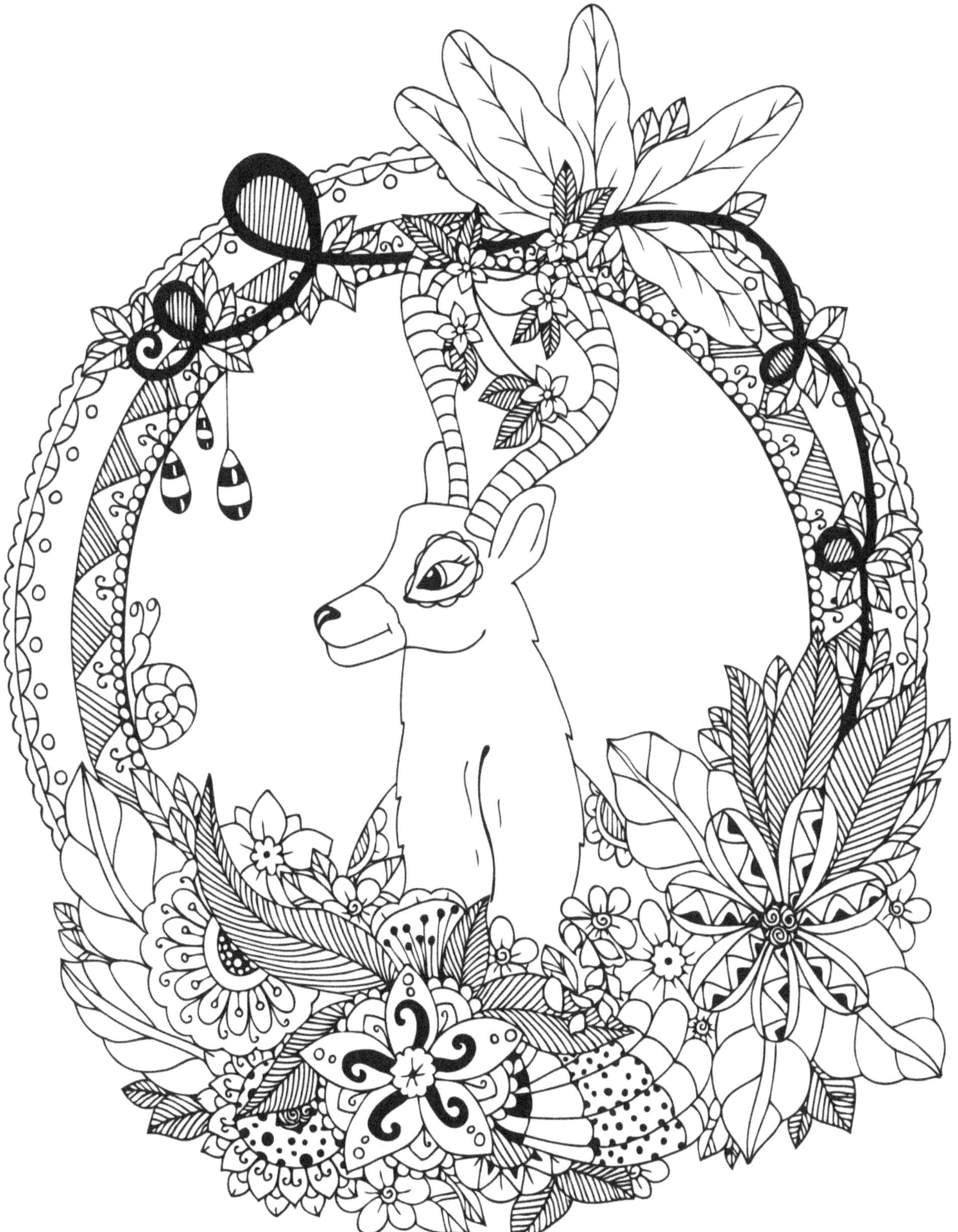

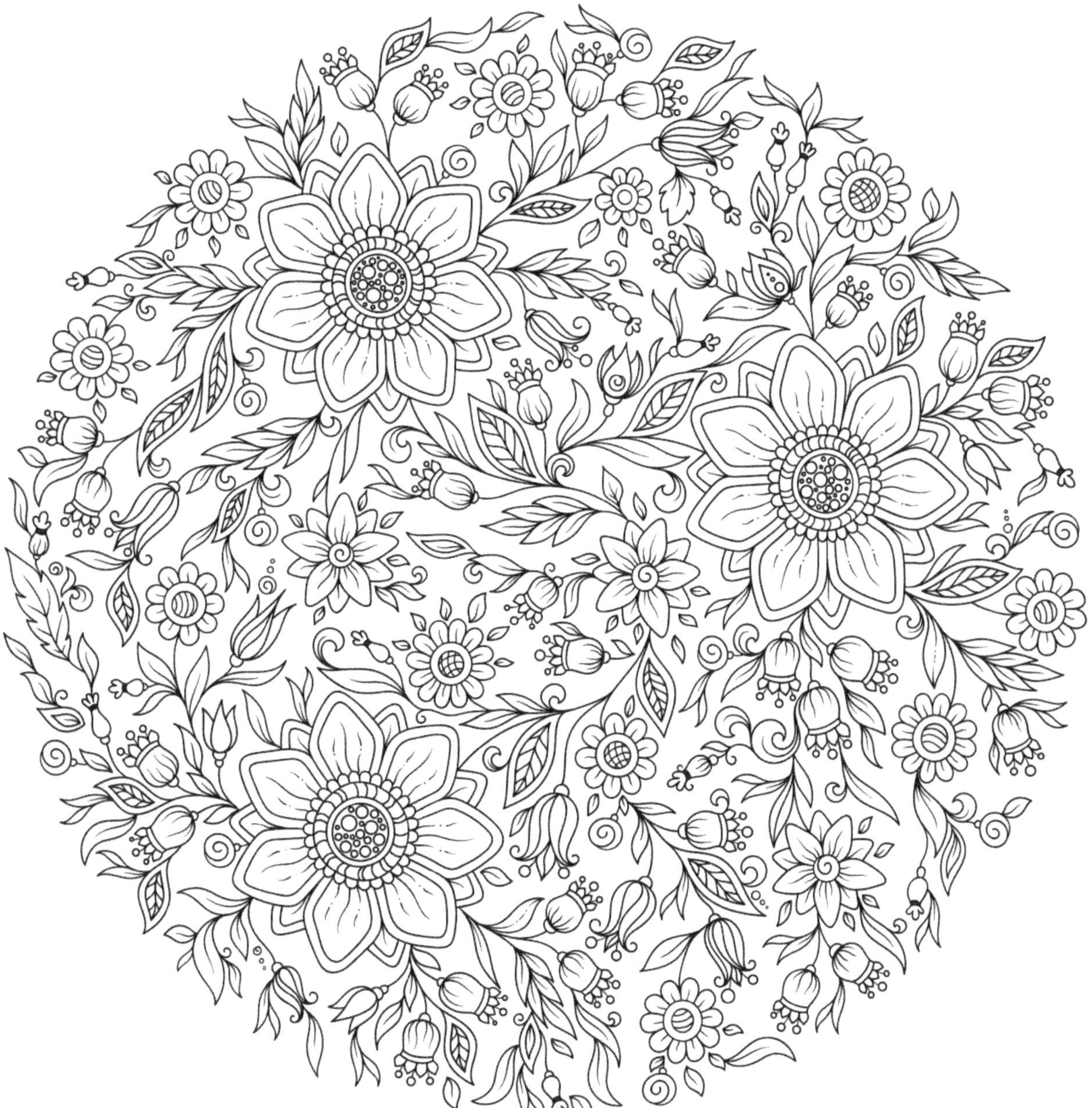

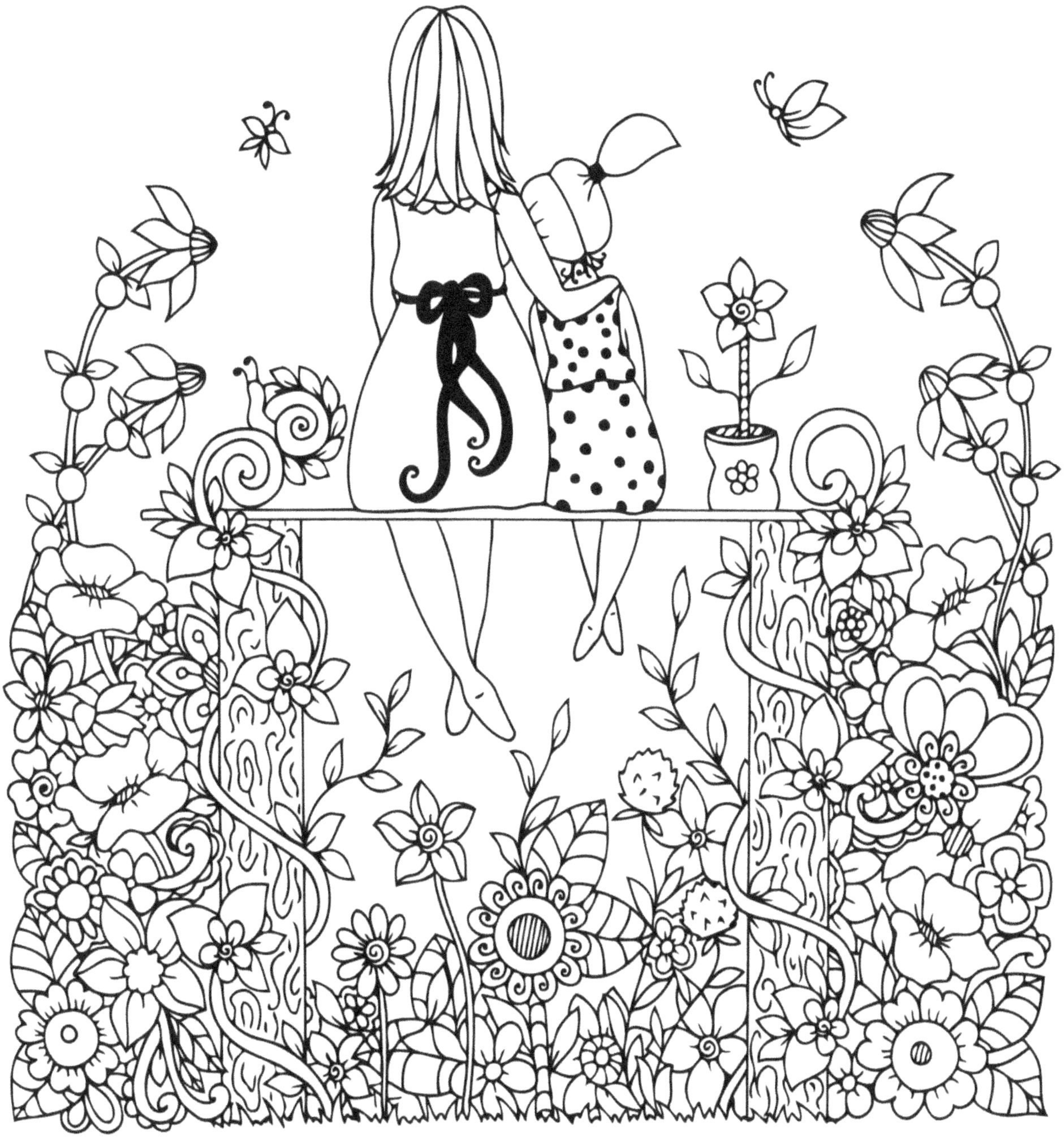

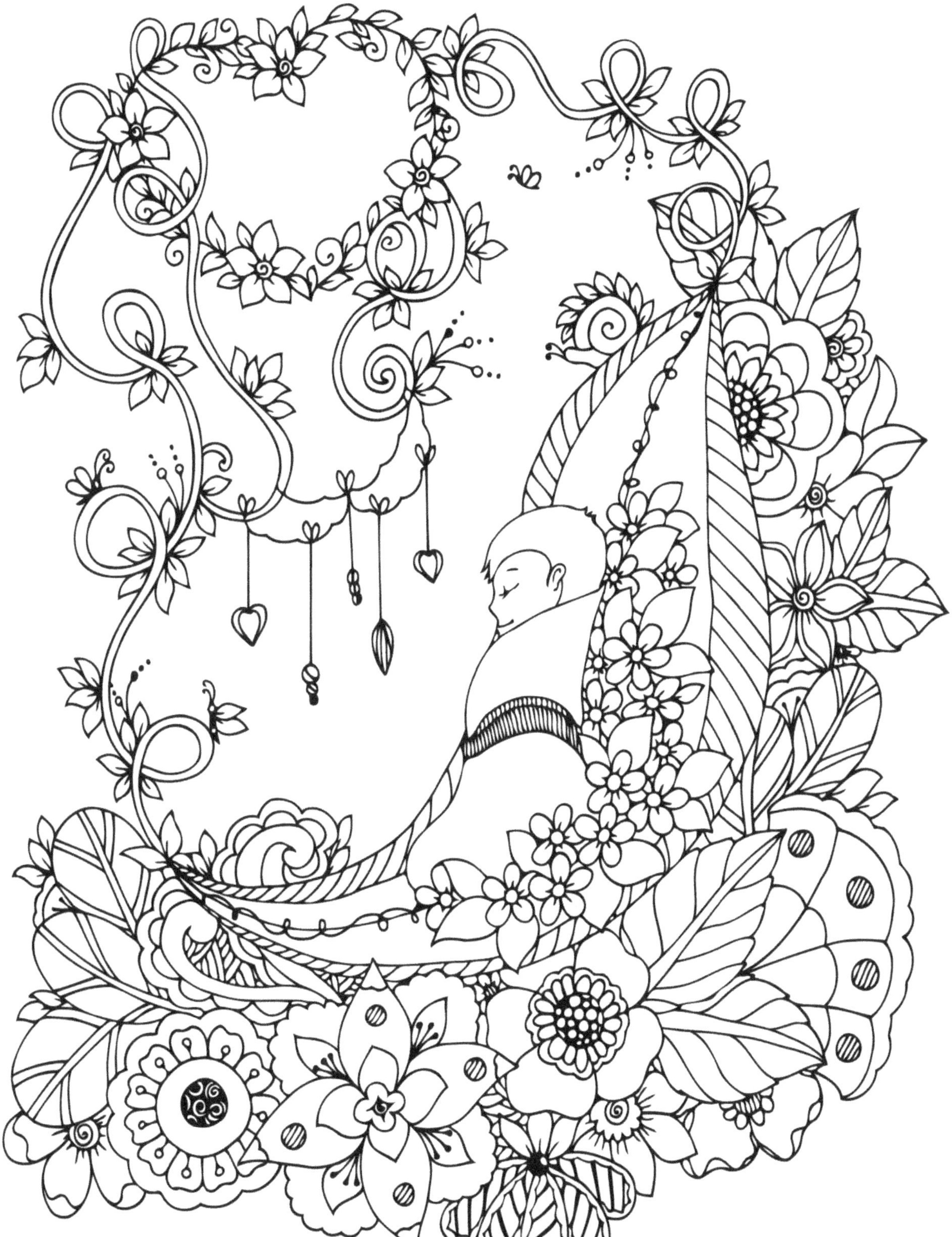

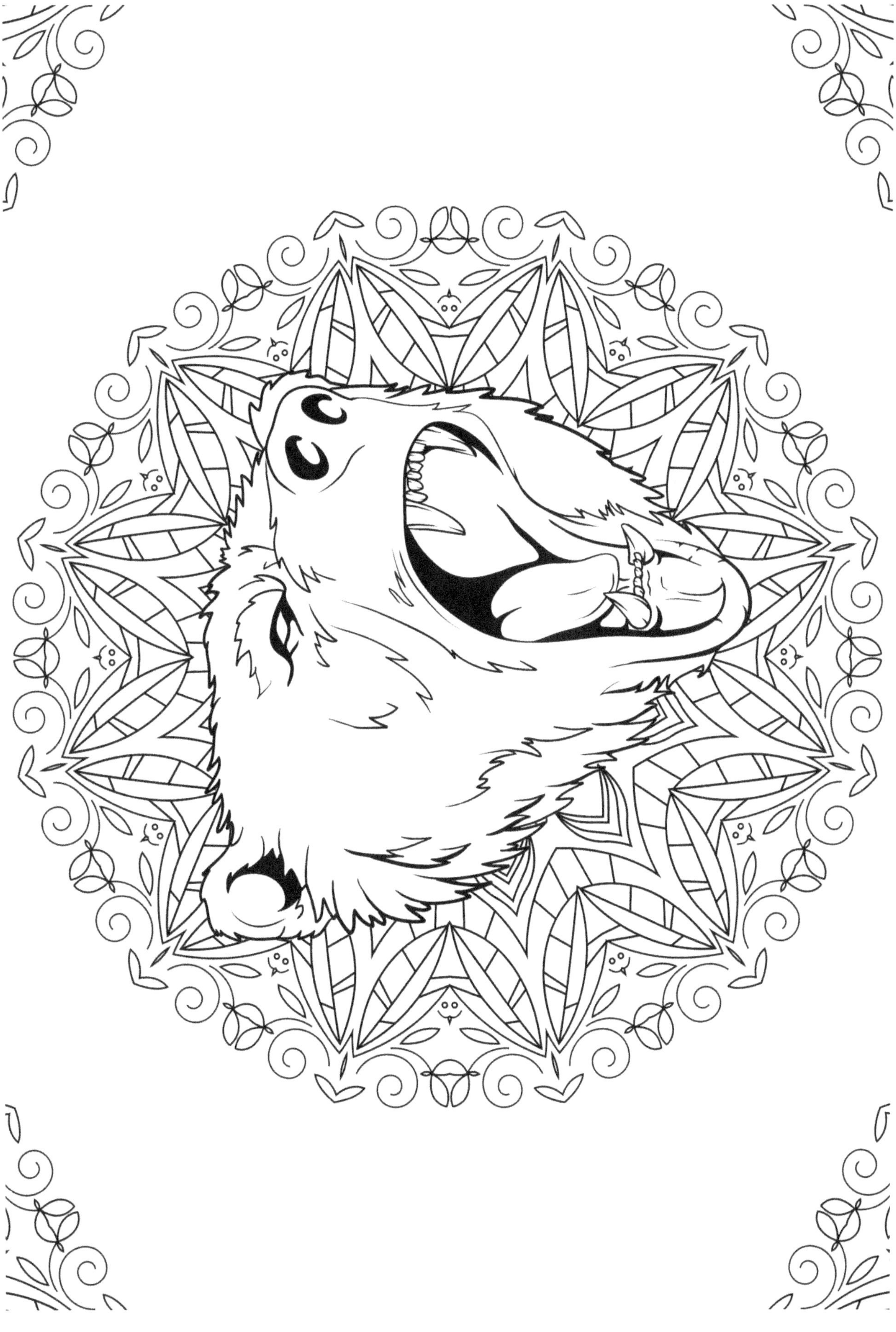

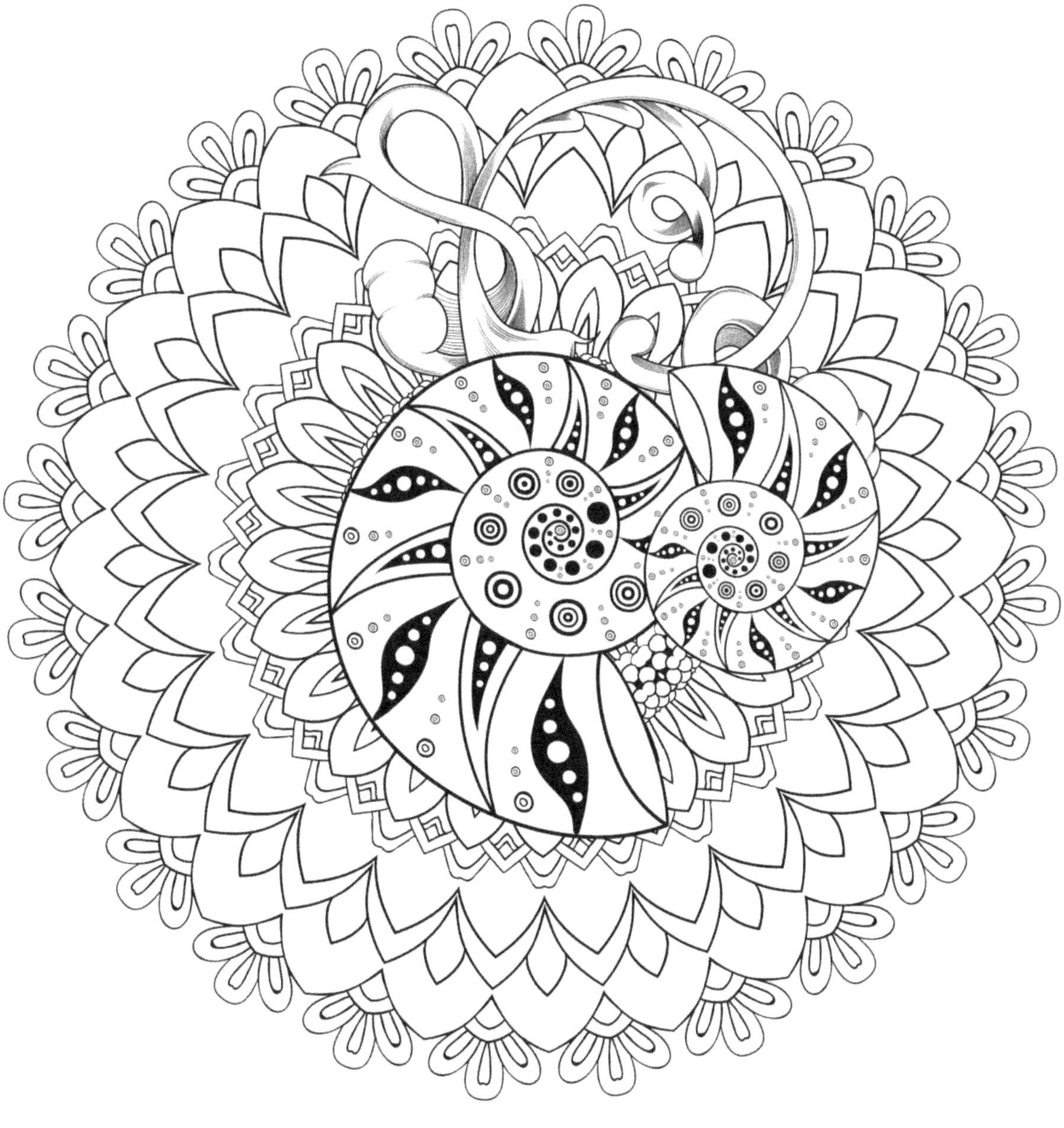

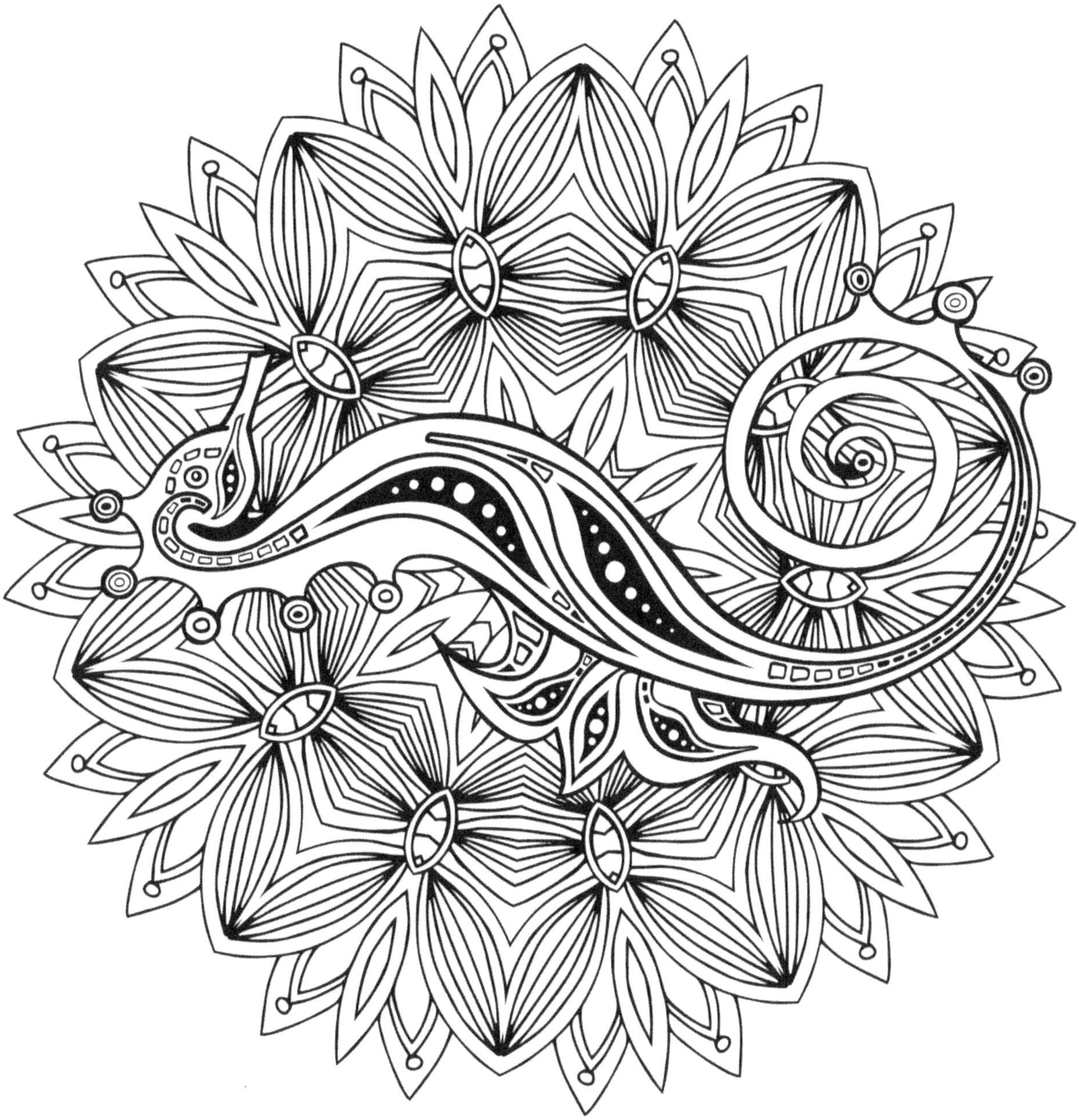

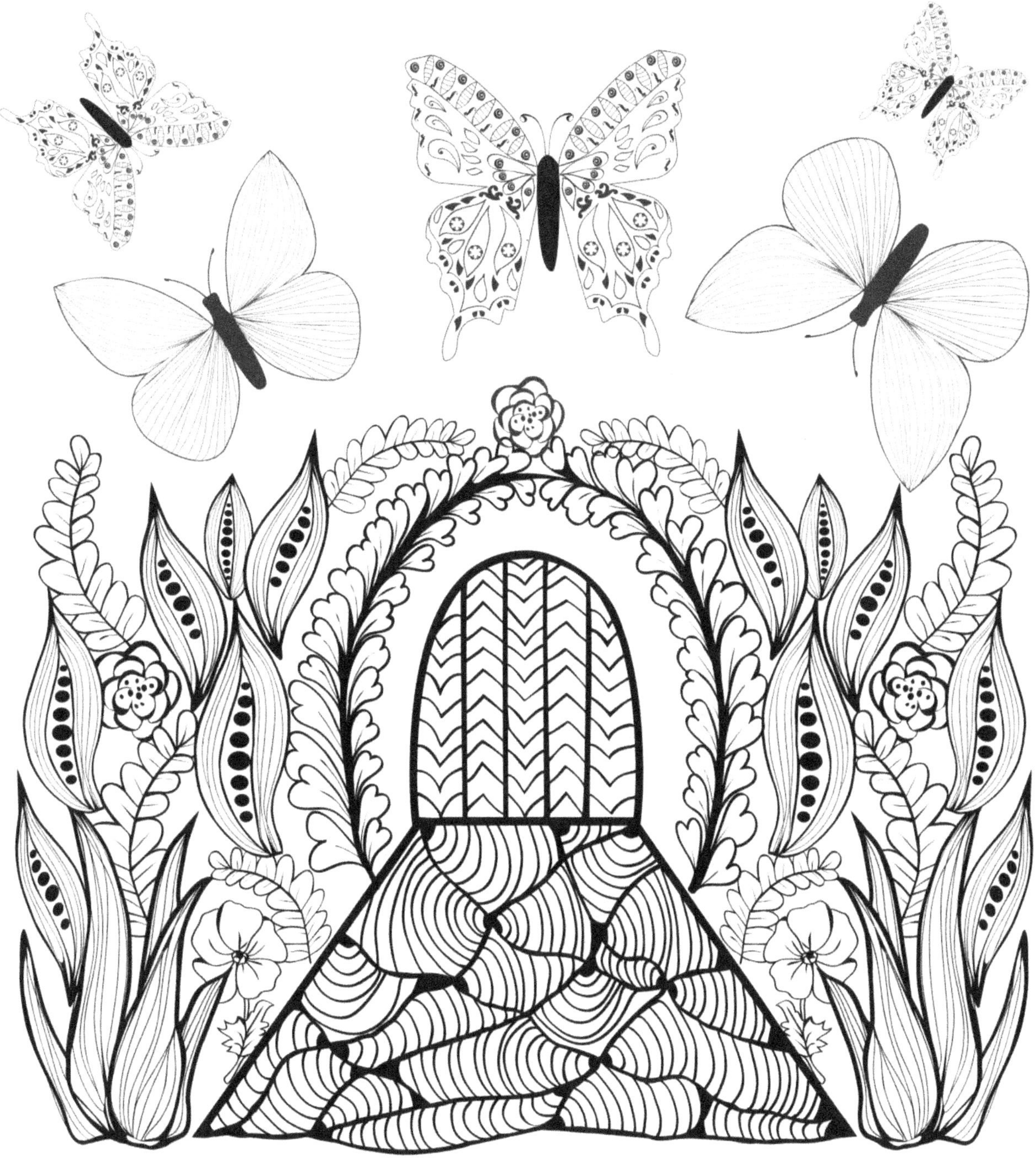

www.ingramcontent.com/pod-product-compliance
Lightning Source LLC
Chambersburg PA
CBHW081252180526
45170CB00007B/2399